Professor Sir John Byers by Henrietta Rae (c 1903), oil on canvas 142cm x 109cm Collection of Queen's University Belfast

SAYINGS, PROVERBS,

AND

HUMOUR OF ULSTER

SIR JOHN WILLIAM BYERS, M.A., M.D.

BOOKS ULSTER

First published by the author in 1904 and printed by William Strain & Sons, Great Victoria Street, Belfast.

This new edition published in 2014

Typographical arrangement, design, layout © Books Ulster

ISBN   978-0-9543063-8-0

CONTENTS

iii

FOREWORD

IT is now more than a century since *Sayings, Proverbs and Humour of Ulster* was first published and copies of the original book have become extremely difficult to obtain. This new edition, with reset text and a few minor corrections, has been produced in order to make the work accessible to a new generation of enthusiasts for Ulster language and folklore.

Some of the words, terms and sayings covered by Byers have survived and are still in common use, but social change over the intervening years has taken its toll on others. For example, words like *quare*, *blether* and *brave* (in the sense of 'very') continue to be widely used and understood, but the term 'Morgan Rattler' (referring to a fast horse) has understandably become obsolete; as the motor car gradually replaced the horse as the normal mode of transport this was practically inevitable.

For the most part, what has been lost cannot be regained, but the republication of books such as this will help prevent the meanings of words and phrases from past literature falling into complete obscurity. They will become the keys which will enable future generations to unlock the trove of their rich social and linguistic heritage.

Sir John Byers was an eminent medical professional in his day and evidently a most industrious man, yet details of his life remain surprisingly sparse. The *British Medical Journal*, for its part, has kindly given consent to the reproduction of the obituary published in its October 2nd, 1920 issue in which some salient details of Sir John's life are given.

Derek Rowlinson,

Bangor,

June 2014

OBITUARY.

Sir JOHN W. BYERS, M.A., M.D., M.A.O.,

Professor of Midwifery, Queen's University of Belfast.

IT was with very deep regret that we announced last week the death of Sir John Byers, which took place on September 20th at his residence, Dreenagh House, Belfast. He had recently returned from a five weeks' holiday in Scotland, and was in excellent health and spirits; he was distressed on learning of the death of his close personal friend and colleague, Mr. Robert Campbell, F.R.C.S.Eng., of whose skill he had availed himself on more than one occasion for his own family. He attended the meeting of the board of management of the Royal Victoria Hospital on September 15th, and moved the vote of condolence in a feeling speech. Subsequently he motored home, and was observed to be ill on arriving at his own door; and the signs of a right hemiplegia with loss of speech and subsequent deepening unconsciousness pointed clearly to cerebral haemorrhage. He sank rapidly on the 19th and died the following evening.

John William Byers was the only child of the late Rev. John Byers, M.A., missionary to China, and of the late Mrs. Margaret Byers, LL.D., founder and principal of Victoria College, Belfast, distinguished for her efforts to promote the higher education of women. He was born in Shanghai in 1853, and so was in his 67th year. He was educated at the Royal Academical Institution, Belfast, and had a brilliant collegiate and university course in Queen's College and University, gaining a gold medal and first honours in his B.A. and M.A. degrees, and honours with his M.D. He studied also in Dublin and in London, where he formed a friendship with the late Sir Jonathan Hutchinson and others. Settling in Belfast, he was appointed to the Belfast Hospital for Sick Children; and in 1882 was appointed as gynaecologist to the new department of the old Royal Hospital, which he organized so successfully. In this he had at first only four beds; in the new Royal Victoria Hospital he left the department with a well-equipped large ward, small ward, operating theatre, and out-patient rooms for the assistant. He was on the active staff for thirty-seven years, a member of the building committee of the new hospital, chairman of the medical staff for three years, and finally, on reaching the age limit, was appointed consultant. His colleagues on his retirement presented him with a Chippendale silver salver containing their autographs. He was also one of the active medical staff to the Belfast Maternity Hospital; and evidence of his recent energy is forthcoming in a short series of consecutive Caesarean sections, all successful, and two successful operations for ruptured uterus during the last year.

Sir John Byers was examiner in obstetrics in the old Royal University of Ireland, and was appointed professor of midwifery and diseases of women in Queen's College. He was a member of the Central Midwives Board for Ireland, having been elected by the medical practitioners resident in Ireland. He was honorary president of the International Congress of Obstetrics and Gynaecology in 1896; vice-president of the Obstetrical Society of London from 1899 to 1901; president of the Ulster Medical Society in 1893-94; president of the North of Ireland Branch of the British Medical Association, 1900-1; president of the Belfast Branch of the Irish Medical Association, 1903-9; president of the Section of Obstetric Medicine and Gynaecology at the meeting of the British Medical Association in Cheltenham, 1901, and delivered the address in obstetrics when the Association held its annual meeting in Belfast in 1909; president of the Section of Physical Education and Training in Personal Hygiene at the International Congress on School Hygiene in London in 1907; president of the Conference on Hygiene of Childhood, in connexion with the Royal Sanitary Congress at Belfast in 1911, and president of the Belfast County Borough Medical Committee in 1912-13. He was one of the two representatives of Ulster on the Council of the British Medical Association, and in 1905, when the Irish Committee was constituted, he was unanimously elected chairman.

Sir John Byers had many and varied interests; amongst these he was a diligent student of the folklore and dialect of Ulster, and was busily engaged during the last few years in the preparation of a book on the subject; he was one of the referees for the province in connexion with the *Oxford Dialect Dictionary*; and nothing pleased him more than to get into conversation with some countryman from an out-of-the-way district and learn his feelings, beliefs, and speech. In 1894* a number of his friends presented him with his portrait in oils, together with a replica for his wife; the former was hung in the Examination Hall of the College. He was always in the forefront in all matters of public health, and showed himself a clear and convincing speaker and a keen debater; one always knew on which side he was in a controversy, and he was a

---

* The obituary in the *Northern Whig,* September 21, 1920, states that the portrait was presented to him in 1906 in recognition of his knighthood 'and of his long and valuable services to public institutions'.

loyal and staunch friend; the students will miss a stimulating influence in the school, and the profession a protagonist who stood for its welfare and high interests. The amount of work he got through was enormous, and the range of his contributions and his activities has become, one may say, proverbial. Although he could not stand shuffling or underhand meanness, and exposed them ruthlessly, yet he had a kind heart and was ever ready to help the young medical man in his struggles; his last act of paying tribute to the worth of a dead colleague was a fit ending to his labours.

He is survived by Lady Byers and three sons, with whom deep sympathy is felt.

[Source: *British Medical Journal*, October 2, 1920].

SAYINGS, PROVERBS, AND HUMOUR OF ULSTER.†

IT has been truly said that nothing is so descriptive and characteristic of a distinct race as their sayings, proverbs, and humour; for a study of these features enables us to form some opinion of the history and character of the people, to understand their habits and peculiarities, to investigate their methods of speech, and, in some measure, to explain why it is they have exerted such an influence on the world's history.

For three hundred years there has existed in Ulster (and mainly in the north-eastern part of that province) a race of people who, by their power of work, level-headedness, and thorough self-reliance, have made Belfast the great centre of Irish industries, have contributed to all parts

† Lecture delivered in part to the members of the Belfast Natural History and Philosophica [sic] Society, December 1st, 1903.

of the British Empire men distinguished in commerce, science, literature, statesmanship, and the arts of war; and, as pointed out by President Roosevelt in his great work, "The Winning of the West," have done so much in colonizing what was formerly called the western states of America—those lying beyond the Alleghanies. Speaking of these settlers from the North of Ireland, President Roosevelt says:

"They did not begin to come to America in any numbers till after the opening of the eighteenth century; but by 1730 they were fairly swarming across the ocean, for the most part in two streams—the larger going to the port of Philadelphia; the smaller to the port of Charleston. Pushing through the long settled lowlands of the sea-coast, they at once made their abode at the foot of the mountains, and became the outposts of civilization. From Pennsylvania, whither the great majority had come, they drifted south along the foothills and down the long valleys till they met their brethren from Charleston, who had pushed up into the Carolina back country. In this land of hills, covered by unbroken forest, they took root and flourished, stretching in a broad belt from north to south, a shield of sinewy men, thrust in between the people of the seaboard and the red warriors of the wilderness. All through this region they were alike; they had as little kinship with the Cavalier as with the Quaker. The west was won by those who have been rightly called the Roundheads of the South, the same men who, before any others, declared for American independence. That these Irish Presbyterians were a bold and hardy race is proved by their at once pushing past the settled regions and plunging into the wilderness as the leaders of the white advance. They were the first and last set of immigrants to do this; all others have merely followed in the wake of their predecessors. But, indeed, they were fitted to be Americans from the very start: they were kinsfolk of the Covenanters; they deemed it a religious duty to interpret their own Bible; and held for a Divine right the election of their own clergy. For generations their whole ecclesiastic and scholastic systems had been fundamentally democratic. In the hard life of the frontier they lost much of their religion, and they had but scant opportunity to give their children the schooling in which they believed; but what few meeting-houses and schools were on the borders were theirs."

The northern Irish are a mixed people, and the Ulsterman, from his heredity, is a product by himself. Through his veins there courses a stream of Scotch, English, French Huguenot, and Irish blood, and so, in the same individual you may sometimes find the pluck and grit of the Englishman, the tenacity and forethought of the Scot, the industry of the Huguenot, with the keen sympathy, pugnacity, and ready wit of the native Irishman.

The predominant element in this racial amalgam is Scottish; and as those who came originally from that country were from both the Lowlands and Highlands, they contributed both Saxon and Celtic elements; but the Ulster race is now, and has been for a lengthened period, as distinct from the Scotch as the American race is from the English. As the late Lord Dufferin— one of the greatest Ulstermen of the nineteenth century, who was in part a Scotchman (his ancestors, the Hamiltons and Blackwoods, came from that country)—once wittily remarked in a St. Andrew's Day speech in India, when he was Governor-General, "Ulstermen were Scotchmen improved by three hundred years' residence in Ireland." The Ulsterman is a true Irishman, proud of his birthplace and of his race.

The characteristics of a race so constituted find expression in the quaint sayings, proverbs, and humour of the people of the northern province of Ireland, which are inspired more by a shrewd observation of men and nature than by mere book learning. They are met with in their most pronounced form among those living in the country districts, as distinguished from the towns; and the clergy and the members of the medical profession who are brought into intimate relationship with the people, hear them most frequently. It is in the plain, homely, everyday talk of the people that you meet these sayings, and as shown by Mr. James N. Richardson, of Bessbrook, if you know your "Ulster," and can handle it properly, you have a language in which you may freely converse in any country in the world, except the northern Irish province, without being "understanded of the people." The use of these quaint sayings is as characteristic of the Ulsterman as his accent, or as his curt, abrupt, and matter-of-fact delivery of his words; and we must never forget, as pointed out by a great writer, that "a countryman is as warm in fustian as a king in velvet; and a truth is as comfortable in homely words as in fine speech." Many of those recorded in this communication I have picked up when professionally engaged in different parts of Ulster. The majority are essentially Ulster in their origin or in their adoption; others have been probably introduced at various times, and may still be met with in other parts of the United Kingdom. The explanation of some of the sayings is at times difficult, and often gives rise to plenty of discussion. Here are three expressions used in Ulster, the origin of which the average reader would have difficulty in finding: "The rale McKay," "A Morgan Rattler," and "Tibb's Eve."

The expression, "The rale McKay," originated in the Highlands, in the country north of Sutherland, where the real home of the great clan

McKay is found. There "The real McKay" is one who is able to claim that both his parents and grandparents (on both sides) were McKays, and so his clan connection is beyond doubt or dispute. The MacKay clan was so famous for its integrity, uprightness, and honesty that its name passed into a proverb in the rest of Scotland, and so to all Scotchmen, "The real MacKay," applied to any person or thing, means that it is genuine and honest, without any shoddy. A blend of Scotch whiskey is advertised as "The real MacKay," and in shops in Glasgow you will see articles labelled "The real MacKay."

In various parts of Ulster the term, "The real MacKay" is used in this sense as indicating that the person or thing so designated is of the very best quality, but in North Antrim the term undoubtedly took its origin in another way. Seven brothers of the MacKay (MacCay) clan came from Ayrshire, and settled at Mosside and Ballintoy, and in the graveyard of the celebrated Franciscan Friary of Bun-na-Margie, near Ballycastle, in North Antrim, so intimately associated with the family of MacDonnell, Earls of Antrim, which, in his most interesting account of this ecclesiastical antiquity, Mr. Francis Joseph Bigger thinks was probably founded in the fourteenth century, there is a stone with heraldic bearings. The arms of the MacKay clan are boldly cut on the west side of this gravestone, while on the east side is the inscription: "Here Lyeth ye Body of Daniel McKay, who Died April ye 2nd, 1732, Aged 30 Years." One of the sons or grandsons of the seven brothers entered the service of a Spanish king and became a distinguished General, and, owing to the services he rendered, he was rewarded by getting the title "Real," which is the Spanish corruption of "Regalis," and indicates a high position in the Casa Real, or royal household. This distinguished General came back with this title, which the country folk pronounced "Rale," and he and his descendants were distinguished from the other McKays in this particular way. It is simply a title of honour pronounced in a peculiar fashion, and with a meaning attached to it different from its original signification. A doctor and a clergyman in North Antrim are descendants of one of the seven original MacKays, and a medical student of Queen's College, Belfast, who graduated M.B. in 1901 is, I am informed, a great-great-great-grandson of one of the seven. The descendants of the General who obtained the Spanish title, are generally supposed to be extinct.

Let me give another expressive phrase from South Down. Many years ago if anyone in that part of Ulster owned a fast horse, it was styled a "Morgan Rattler." The same term was applied, in coursing, to a hare which the greyhounds failed to catch, such as the type described in that striking book published recently, "The Confessions of a

Poacher," or to a quick runner among schoolboys. I chanced to lend some time ago to a County Down gentleman "The Life of General Chesney," one of the most distinguished men that the "Kingdom of Mourne" has produced, and, in returning it, he told me he had made a great find which explained the term "Morgan Rattler," for the biography showed that the "Morgan Rattler" was a famous armed smuggling lugger which frequented the Mourne shores, and in General Chesney's life (p. 34), an account is given of an encounter between the daring crew of this celebrated boat and the Revenue men, of whom General Chesney's father was captain, or coast officer. This ship was so quick and hard to catch that anything with similar qualities was designated a "Morgan Rattler," or was said to be as fleet as the "Morgan Rattler."

"Tibb's Eve."—This is an Ulster way of designating a day which will never come. Like the millenium [sic] or the "Greek Kalends" it indicates an indefinite or unfixed period of time, and so is really an evasion. One often hears in Ulster the expression: "He'll pay ye on Tibb's Eve," or, "Ye'll get it again Tibb's Eve," which means, you will be paid, or will get something on a day which will never come; and you also find it in the phrase: "Tibb's Eve is the day neither afore (before) Christmas nor after." But what is Tibb? and how did the saying come to be so common in Ulster? Some authorities say it is a corruption of Saint Ubes, which again is a corruption of Setuval. Now, as there is no such saint in the calendar, the eve falls practically on "the Greek Kalends." Other authorities think Tibb, Tibbia, etc., are corruptions of the name Isabel; but as there is no such saint immortalized, the responsibility of one promising to do anything on "Tibb's Eve" is obvious. A third explanation is that St. Tibb's evening is the evening of the last day, or Day of Judgment, and so one understands the meaning of being paid on "Tibb's Eve." All these explanations are unsatisfactory. The term, which is a very old one, was probably imported into Ulster, but when, and by whom, there is no accurate information.

When an Ulsterman, on buying an article, pays at once, he is said to "pay on the nail." This curious phrase, which is the antithesis of "tick" (abbrev. of ticket), was thought by some to owe its origin to the fact that money was paid on a counter studded with nails; but two other explanations have been put forward:

1st.—In a Parliamentary Deed of King Robert the Bruce, it is stipulated by indenture, dated July 15th, 1326 ("Scots Acts," I. 476), that a tenth penny was covenanted for, payable to the King. On his part, he agreed not to exact certain horses and carriages unless he was passing through the realm, after the custom of his predecessor, Alexander III., for which horses and carriages full payment should be made *super unguem*, that is, "down on the nail," or into the hand, "*solvere super unguem*."

2nd.—O'Keefe, in his "Recollections," Vol I., speaking of the period 1773-5, writes: "During the Limerick Assizes I saw a stuffed glove, about four feet long, hanging out from the top of the exchange, nearly across the main street; this was the accustomed token that for a week or fortnight, whilst the courts were sitting, no debtor could be arrested. . . . An ample piazzo under the exchange was a thoroughfare, in the centre stood a pillar four feet high, upon it a circular plate of copper about three feet in diameter, this was called the nail, and on it was paid the earnest for any commercial bargain made, which was the origin of the saying, 'paid down on the nail.' " The "nail" existed at Bristol, Liverpool, and other places in England. It is probable it was through the first or Scotch origin that the term "on the nail" came to be used in Ulster. In Fletcher's "Spanish Curate" we find it:

"What legacy would you bequeathe me now,
    And *pay it on the nail* to fly my fury?"

and in the following very witty poem by a distinguished townsman of Belfast, the late Dr. J. S. Drennan:

AGAINST LEGACIES TO DOCTORS.

"No, no, ma'am, this legacy plan would soon
  fail,
    Whatever goodwill it attests;
Let the curer of bodies be *paid on the nail,*
    To the saver of souls leave bequests.

"Your doctor endow, whilst he keeps you alive,
    With guineas in proof of his merit,
But take my advice, if you wish to survive,
    And nought let him hope to inherit.

"Medicines sometimes are pois'nous, post-obit
  fees
    Might make Aesculapius death's proctor;
And bad enough surely to die of disease,
    'Twere the devil to die of the doctor."

Dr. J. Swanwick Drennan was son of the
celebrated Dr. William Drennan, who was born
and died in Belfast, and who wrote many pieces.
In one of them, "Erin," is the famous phrase, "The
Emerald Isle." After the death of Dr. J. Swanwick
Drennan, his children published, in loving
remembrance, a volume of his charming "Poems
and Sonnets." It is from a copy of this book,
given me by his nephew, the Right Hon. Thomas
Andrews, D.L., that I quote several pieces in this
paper. Dr. J. S. Drennan was a man of the highest

literary culture, and a great favourite with those who were privileged to enjoy his friendship. Of a retiring nature, his rather sad and even melancholy appearance was a curious environment for a man possessed of the keenest sense of humour.

In Ulster certain words are often employed peculiarly; for example, the word "disorder" is used for a disease or illness, generally of an infectious nature, and the same term is applied to an outbreak among animals (pigs, etc.). In recent years one has heard in Ulster the influenza described as a most "sevendible (severe or seven double) disorder." Shakespeare, in King John, employs it rather as indicating a sort of temporary mental aberration:

"I will not keep this form upon my head,
When there is such *disorder* in my wit."

It is also employed as a weaker term than disease, to imply functional disturbance without structural changes, as is well seen in the following lines by Dr. J. S. Drennan:

MEDICAL RECIPE.

"By a patient too fair sat a doctor too young,
With eyes more intent on her lips than her
tongue;
He tested her heart, as its pulse's recorder,

But, alas! in his own was the latent disorder;
And soon from the region in which it was bred,
This sad "tremor cordis" so muddled his head,
That instead of some physic to mend her
    condition,
He urged as a recipe, take your physician."

When an Ulsterman is suffering from a malady which is attended with paroxysms of pain, he says the pain comes in "stoons," or he may say he has a "stooning" in the part affected, as his side, head, etc. This word is apparently a contraction of stound, a very old English noun, meaning a severe blow or stroke, and is connected with stound, an old past participle of stun, itself a variant of stunned. The word is akin to the Sanskrit stan=sound, thunder. Spenser, in the "Faery Queen," uses both, the noun:

"Like to a mazed steare
That yet of mortal stroke, the *stound* doth
    beare";

and the verb:

"So was he *stound* with stroke of her huge taile."

The word is also allied to astound. It is interesting therefore to know that when a County Down, County Derry, or County Tyrone man says he has "stoons" of pain, instead of being accused, as is sometimes the case, of using a vulgar word, he is employing one of the oldest and most expressive terms in our language.

Those who have suffered from a disease like influenza know the extraordinary condition of weakness, depression, and general absence of very high self-appreciation which often follows that complaint. In such circumstances the American says "he feels vary mean," the Englishman puts it, "You could hang me over a clothes' line"; how much more expressive was the saying of the Ulsterwoman who, describing the condition of her child in such circumstances, said to the physician at an hospital where she went for advice, "I could lap (an old word, from which the more modern wrap, a doublet of lap, is derived) her roun' my wee finger."

Lap in this sense means to "twist round," but it is also used with the idea of "to cover something underneath," or to "muffle," as in the following exquisite lyric of William Allingham:

HALF WAKING.

"I thought it was the little bed
    I slept in long ago;
A straight, white curtain at the head,
    And two smooth knobs below.

"I thought I saw the nursery fire,
    And in a chair well known

My mother sat, and did not tire
  With reading all alone.

"If I should make the slightest sound
    To show that I'm awake,
She'd rise, and *lap* the blankets round,
    My pillow softly shake;

"Kiss me, and turn my face to see
    The shadows on the wall,
And then sing Rousseau's dream to me,
    Till fast asleep I fall.

"But this is not my little bed;
    That time is far away;
'Mong strangers cold I live instead,
    From dreary day to day."

When hay is cut, armfuls are often rolled up in such a way as to form conical heaps, which "turn" the rain. Each of these is called in Ulster a "lap-cole." Lap here conveys the idea of folding one part over another, while "cole" is derived from the Icelandic kollr=a top, a head, a heap. The English dialectical variant of it is "coil," as in "Child's Ballads":

"O bonny, bonny, sang the bird,
  Sat in the *coil* o' hay."

In walking or running matches, a single round

of the course is a "lap." In America what is called
in our country a travelling rug is designated a "lap-
robe." Wrap, hap, and lap are closely associated,
and one of the ways they are employed conveys
the idea of protecting from cold. In Ulster, as well
as in Scotland and the North of England, a "hap"
is a cloak, plaid, or covering.

A lady suffering from a sudden brain attack
said to me most expressively: "I'm moithered,"
meaning her head was confused. This word is
allied to muddle. In "Corymeela," [sic] by Moira
O'Neill, the native of the glen, in speaking of the
place he is living in in England, says:

"This livin' air is moithered wi' the bummin'
o' the bees" (bummin': an imitative word, the
earlier representation of the modern booming. A
man who boasts is said in Ulster to be "bummin'
" "blowing," "bragging," or "breezing." The
American words are "booming": "Business is
booming"; "boomer"—one who assists in a boom;
and in "Silas Marner," George Eliot uses the word
as indicating distracted: "You'll happen to be a bit
moithered with it (a child) while it's so little."

A person who cannot endure pain well is
said in Ulster to be a bad "tholer." The word thole
(early English, tholen; Anglo-Saxon, tholian;
old Saxon, tholean; Icelandic, thola; Greek,
tolman=suffer: Latin, tolerare=tollere—hence
tolerate) in this sense of bearing injuries silently,
or enduring torture (mental or physical) without

word or complaint, is an extremely old one. In "Piers Plowman" we have it used:

"And what myschief and malese Cryst for man tholed."

The following Ulster proverb, "Thole weel's a fine cowlt" (colt), means that patience and endurance go far. It is also employed in another sense, meaning to wait, as the following story will illustrate. Many years ago there lived in the district of Rathfriland, County Down (a locality which has given birth to so many able women and men), a clergyman who was clever, popular, and humorous. On one occasion, while engaged in baptizing a child, he enquired from the father the name of the infant. The parent for a moment forgot what the child was to be named, and in his confusion, while scratching his head, said: "Thole a wee, sir" (meaning, wait a little), whereupon the minister continued, "Thole a wee, I baptize thee," but was suddenly interrupted by the father, who had now recollected the name, exclaiming: "Oh, stop, sir, the child's name's Hugh!"

Strangers coming to reside in Ulster are at first puzzled at the way "better" is used in regard to a person who is ailing. If you ask an Ulsterman how a relative is who you have heard is very ill, and, in reply, he says, "he is better," it does not mean simply that the person has got the "turn" of the disease (as it is termed), but that he is quite recovered.

A mother when harassed with a child who is constantly crying says she is "heart-scalded," and so a member of a family or connection who is a constant source of trouble is termed a "heart's scald." Some think this expressive word is "heart's scold," "scald" being Scotch for "scold," as in the "Taming of the Shrew," Petruchio says: "I know she is an irksome brawling scold," but I believe the word is "heart scald," that is, someone who, by their actions, affects painfully, or scalds, the heart=a "heart break."

A place where rowdy characters collect is termed a "randy-boose." A friend walking through Holywood heard someone in the street say of a place where there was a collection of corner-boys: "That's a regular randy-boose for all the roughs." It is often applied to a race-course. One explanation of this phrase is that it is a corruption of "rendez-vous," the word coming from the French through Scotland. I believe, however, it is a compound of two words, "randy," a Scotch word=disorderly or boisterous (in the "Jolly Beggars" Burns writes:

"A merry core
O' randie gangrel bodies ").

and "boose," a very old word (Anglo-Saxon, bos; Icelandic, bass; Danish, bass), meaning a stall or enclosure for cattle (cows or horses). The word "boose" dates back to the fifteenth century when it was first used. In various parts of County Down the word "boose" simply means a situation, or post, or office, as the following story will illustrate: In a well-known town in South Down there lived many years ago a lad of great natural ability, who, by the help of a very kindly clergyman, became a member of a learned profession. Unfortunately he at times was unsteady, and in corresponding with him, his friend and patron, the clergyman, thought it advisable to remind him of his failing. It so happened that at this particular time Sir Thomas Larcom was Registrar-General of Ireland, and the clergyman was the local Registrar of Marriages in his own district. One day he had occasion to send a return to that official, while at the same time he wrote a letter to his protege, beginning it, "Dear Tommy" (the same Christian name as that of the Registrar-General), reminding him to keep clear of the drink as he had a "snug *boose,* good pay, and not much to do." Unfortunately, the letters were put into the wrong envelopes, and a most amusing situation arose, when a sharp reprimand came down from Charlemont House, Dublin (the official residence of the Registrar-General), asking for an immediate explanation, and shortly afterwards a note from the young friend to the clergyman enquiring what in all the world he had to do with the registration of marriages. Speaking of "boose" reminds me that in Comber there is an old street (the present High Street) called the Cow "Vennel," a word which is simply the French "venelle"=a small street.

Here are three words applied in Ulster to animals which the semi-educated might in error consider to be vulgar. When a goat is attached to one end of a rope or chain, the other extremity of which is fastened in the ground by means of an iron pin ("stab"), it is said to be "tethered." This is a very old word (formerly "tedder" as used by Bacon: "We live joyfully, going abroad within our tedder"), occurring in old Friesic (tieder), Icelandic (tjodhr), and Danish (toir), and Gaelic (teadhir=a tether). A horse, two of whose legs are bound together, generally on the same side, is said to be "langeled." This is an old English word, meaning to bind together or "hobble" a horse. "Lanyel" is a variant. If a valuable hen, or especially one with a brood of young birds, breaks one of her legs, a splinter of wood is carefully bound to one side of the leg, as a surgeon uses a splint in setting a broken bone, and the hen, who manages to walk about in this condition, is said to be "spelcheled." The word "spelch," which is the same as "spelk," is a very old one (middle English, spelke; Anglo-Saxon, spelc; Danish, spalk; Icelandic, spelkur), meaning, to set, as a broken bone, with a splint or spelk (a splinter of wood). I have often heard people in the country speak of a splint used by surgeons as a "splinter."

In County Armagh, food that is insipid is termed "wersh," a word which is probably of Scotch origin. It is also applied to a person of pale or sickly appearance. We find in "Old Mortality," "*Wersh* parritch, neither good to fry, boil, nor sup cauld." In the "History First Forty Years," Vol. I., p. 242, Carlyle writes: "Irving and she are sometimes ridiculous enough at present in the matter of their son, a quiet *wersh* gorb of a thing, as all children of six weeks are." And in "Life in London," Vol. I., p. 244, he says: "I went to the factor as I proposed on Friday—a harmless, intelligent enough, rather *wersh* looking man." It may be a reduced form of "wearish," a word of uncertain etymology, but having perhaps relationships with "weary" and "waterish." If the word comes from Scotland its use in Armagh (in which it is common), where there was an early English settlement, is peculiar.

In walking through a bog or "moss" one sometimes, as in shooting snipe, suddenly comes upon a place, where, owing to the marshy, shaking nature of the soil, there is risk of sinking deeply. Such a situation is known in Ulster as a "*Qua*," a word abbreviated from "quag," to which in "Pilgrim's Progress" Bunyan thus refers: "On the left hand there was a very dangerous *quag,* into which, if even a good man falls, he can find no bottom for even his foot to stand on; into that quag King David once did fall." Now this word "quag" is a shortened form of "quagmire," which is a variant of the earlier "quakemire" (old English, quake=shake, and mire=damp, yielding soil). So we have quakemire, quagmire, quag, qua.

The Ulsterman, with all his level-headedness, has a good deal of superstition in his nature, and this becomes specially evident in times of sickness; and so the baying of a dog, the breaking of a looking-glass, or the sudden creaking of a table or chair in a house where anyone is seriously ill, is often regarded as a probable forerunner of death; but if anyone sees, or, rather, imagines he sees, an apparition, then the superstitious are almost certain that death is at hand. I recollect well some years ago driving late at night from Ballycastle to Ballymoney. The jarvey was doing his utmost by constant talking to while away the tedium of this rather tiresome journey, when quite suddenly, as we were passing a place called the "dry arch" (where one country road crosses another by a bridge), he said in a most alarmed manner: "Sir, there's my brother's wraith," pointing with his whip to the side of the road (he had previously mentioned he was ill), and not another word could he be induced to utter until we arrived at Ballymoney. The moon had previously arisen, and probably the silhouette or outline formed by its sudden shining through the trees at the side of the road had convinced him that, as in Tennyson's "Maud":

"Then glided out of the joyous wood
The ghastly *wraith* of one I knew."

Another sign of the Ulsterman's superstition
is the existence throughout the northern province
of fairy lore, more marked in some districts
than in others, but gradually becoming less
prevalent. Among the peasants—especially those
of a superstitious turn of mind—there is a strong
belief that fairies are real and are not to be trifled
with. These little creatures are supposed to be a
sort of intermediate beings between men and
angels. The tradition is that the fairies were at one
time angels in heaven, but were punished for their
pride by being cast out. Some, it is said, fell on the
earth, others into the sea, but a third group were
carried by demons to the nether regions. These
latter are demoniacal, and are used by the evil one
to do wicked deeds. These malicious fairies, it is
said, live under the earth, and impart knowledge
of wicked spells, of magic, and of potions to
certain evil persons chosen by the devil, such
as the witch-women. The fairies who fell into
the sea have palaces under the ocean and ride
on white horses, and often hold revels and have
dances with their companions on the land, who
live in the clefts of the hills, and frequent forths
or raths, and are specially fond of the hawthorn.
The fairies are small in stature, and can render
their bodies invisible and pass them through

all sorts of enclosures. Fair in complexion, they are generally clothed in green; as a rule they are kindly and frolicsome, and very fond of music and dancing, but they may be mischievous or spiteful to human beings, because, while the human race is immortal, the fairies, tradition says, will be annihilated on the last day. They are very particular in their habits, and dislike anyone that is of a mean or niggardly nature, so it is common in some places to leave water for them to wash in, to put some food on the "dresser" (dresser is from the old French dresseur, dreceur, dreçor; modern French, dressoir=a sideboard, and comes from dresser=to dress. In the "Taming of the Shrew," Petruchio says, in reference to the burnt mutton: "How durst you, villains, bring it from the *dresser*") for them to eat; and, curiously, the common custom of placing coom or peat (turf) dust (coom, koom, comb, is a dialect variant of culm, which is derived from the old English culme, colm=soot, smoke, from which came the words, culmy, colmy=black or smutted. Culm became coom as coulter became cooter. The word "coom" apparently comes from Scotland, where its original meaning was soot forming about a fireplace. The "smithy coom" was the hard granular grit which forms over a blacksmith's fire. Then it came to be used for coal dust or slack. In the North of Ireland it is invariably applied to the dust or fine particles of turf) at the back of the kitchen fire, which, while it serves to prevent it going out, is also used among the superstitious with the idea of providing a fire for the fairies, who often hold council, it is said, around it at night. The fox-glove is known as "fairy fingers," and I remember as a boy being shown in the country rings in the fields caused, it was believed, by the fairies dancing in circles. Alas! modern science shows that this phenomenon is due to the growth of certain fungi, which appear in a single night, forming a circle in the grass as if sprinkled with ashes. There is a dread among the country people lest the fairies may carry off their children, and in certain places it is believed they can do so only before the children are baptized, and so the parents watch the cradles most anxiously till they are christened. If the fairies bewitch the children before they are baptized, tradition says, such infants grow up bad and have the "evil eye," and so by their look bring ill-luck. In certain parts of Tyrone, if an infant is taken out "after dark" a little salt is placed in some of its garments (dress or petticoat), probably as a charm against the fairies. The serious part of this is that if the fairies take an infant away "the changeling" they leave, being their own offspring or elve, is believed to be less robust (Tennyson in "The Coming of Arthur" has clearly this idea when he writes: "Shrunk like a fairy changeling lay the mage") and of defective intellect, so that in some places the term "changeling" simply means an idiot. The fairies are believed to inhabit forts or raths as well as underground dwellings, and to have a special predilection for thorns, and a stranger noticing a thornbush growing in the centre of a field or the portion of a rath, and asking why it is not removed, will be told it would annoy the fairies to do so.

Another and more realistic view of the fairies has been put forward by Mr. D. MacRitchie in his book, "The Testimony of Tradition." According to this authority, the fairies, with whom we have been traditionally acquainted, are the mound-dwellers, whose remains have been found in the form of green hillocks, which have, as in one of the most noted, the "Ma'es-How," of Orkney, been artificially erected over a long, low passage, leading to a central chamber, which has no roof, but is open to heaven. Mr. MacRitchie explains, as is well known, that many traditions in fairy folk-lore connect the "good people" with mounds, which subsequent investigation has shown to be the residence of men of a pigmy race. He identifies these with the Picts (fairies are termed in Scotland "Pechs"). There can be no doubt, apart from this theory of MacRitchie's, that in Ulster, as in other places, the stories in reference to fairies are often associated with hills, forts, and subterranean residences (generally of a palatial nature) into which the "wee folk" often suddenly disappear. There is a very interesting discussion of this question in "English Fairy Tales," written by the Editor of "Folk-Lore," Mr. Joseph Jacobs, and illustrated by Mr. John D. Batten. Mr. Jacobs says: "If, as archaeologists tell us, there was once a race of men in Northern Europe, very short and hairy, that dwelt in underground chambers, artificially concealed by green hillocks, it does not seem unlikely that odd survivors of the race should have lived on after they had been conquered and nearly exterminated by Aryan invaders, and should occasionally have performed something like the pranks told of Fairies and Trolls." Mr. MacRitchie's work is a most interesting one, but all the traditions about the fairies existing in our folk-lore cannot be explained in his "realistic" way.

A popular superstition prevails in the Ards district of County Down that John MacAnanty, the Northern Fairy King, lived on Scrabo Hill, and held his court in the interior of the cairn on its summit. The banshee, or woman fairy—the spirit of death—is the most terrible of all the fairy race. The cry of this awful apparition is the most weird and mournful of all earthly sounds, and, heard in the silence of the night, betokens death to some member of a historic family, to whom this spirit is attached. The fairies, being small of stature, are designated as "wee folk," and to propitiate them are called "good folk." Moira O'Neill, whose poetry is so much associated with the Glens of Antrim, in her "Baby Song," writes:

A BABY SONG.

"When my little son is born on a sunny summer
morn,
I'll take him sleepin' in my arms to walk beside
the sea,
For the windy wathers blue would be dancin' if
they knew,
And the weeny waves that wet the sand come
creepin' up to me.

"When my pretty son's awake, och! the care o' him
I'll take,
An' we'll never pass a gentle place between the
dark an' day;
If he's lovely in his sleep on his face a veil I'll keep,
Or the *wee folk* an' the *good folk* might be
wantin' him away.

"When my darlin' comes to me he will lie upon my
knee—
Though the world should be my pillow he must
know no harder place—
Sure a queen's son may be cold in a cradle all o'
gold,
But my arm shall be about him, an' my kiss
upon his face."

"Moira O'Neill" is the well-known *nom-de-
plume* of a member of an old and distinguished

County Antrim family who, at Cushendun, wrote
her first songs and tales of "The Glen Folk" of North
Antrim, and who at present resides in Ireland.
Many of her lyrics have appeared in *Blackwood's
Magazine* (old Mr. Blackwood was one of her early
literary patrons) and in the *Spectator*. She has a
most interesting personal history, in reference to
which I say nothing out of respect to her own wish
to preserve her incognito. No one has done more,
as pointed out by Stephen Gwynn, than "Moira
O'Neill" to redeem English-speaking Ireland from
the reproach of lacking a literature, and no poet
has shown more of the "Celtic note" in her songs;
and I may be allowed to define this "Celtic note"
by quoting the following from a very interesting
paper by Quiller Couch:

"Meanwhile let it be understood that in
speaking of a 'Celtic note' I accuse no fellow-
creature of being an Irishman, Scotsman,
Welshman, Manxman, Cornishman, or Breton.
The poet will as a rule turn out to be one or other
of these, or at least to have a traceable strain of
Celtic blood in him. But to the note only is the
term applied. Now this note (as I shall hope in
some future paper to show) may be recognized
by many tokens; but the first and chiefest is its
insistence upon man's brotherhood with bird and
beast, star and flower, everything in short which
we loosely call 'nature,' his brotherhood even with
spirits and angels, as one of an infinite number of

microcosms reflecting a common image of God. And poetry which holds by this creed will hardly be subservient to societies and governments and legalized doctrines and conventions; it will hold to them by a long and loose chain if at all. It flies high enough, at any rate, to take a bird's eye view of all manner of things which in the temple, the palace, or the market-place have come to be taken as axiomatic. It eyes them with an extraordinary 'dissoluteness,' if you will give that word its literal meaning. It sees that some accepted virtues carry no reflection of heaven; it sees that heaven, on the other hand—so infinite is its care—may shake with anger from bound to bound at the sight of a caged bird. It sees that the souls of living things even of the least conspicuous, reach up by chains and are anchored in heaven, while "great" events slide by on the surface of this skimming planet with empires and their ordinances."

This subject, fairy lore, is a most attractive one to all interested in literature, and, as pointed out by G. A. Greene, "together with its kindred science of mythology and folk-lore, it provides us with the nearest glimpses now obtainable of the primitive imagination of man, upon which almost all imaginative literature, even the greatest, is primarily founded." No writer had a greater sympathy with, and appreciation of, the fairy world of fancy and myth than the Ulster poet Allingham, as is well seen in his charming poems,

"The Fairy King," "The Lepracaun (Leprahaun) or Fairy Shoemaker" (a great favourite in Co. Donegal), and in the well-known child's song:

THE FAIRIES.

"Up the airy mountain,
    Down the rushy glen,
We daren't go a-hunting
    For fear of little men:
Wee folk, good folk,
    Trooping all together,
Green jacket, red cap,
    And white owl's feather!

"Down along the rocky shore
    Some make their home:
They live on crispy pancakes
    Of yellow-tide foam;
Some in the reeds
    Of the black mountain lake,
With frogs for their watch-dogs,
    All night awake.

"High on the hill-top
    The old king sits:
He is now so old and grey,
    He's nigh lost his wits;
With a bridge of white mist
    Columbkill he crosses,

On his stately journeys,
  From Slieveleague to Rosses;
Or going up with music,
  On cold, starry nights,
To sup with the Queen
  Of the gay Northern Lights.

"They stole little Bridget
  For seven years long;
When she came down again
  Her friends were all gone;
They took her lightly back,
  Between the night and morrow,
They thought that she was fast asleep,
  But she was dead with sorrow.
They have kept her ever since,
  Deep within the lake,
On a bed of flag leaves,
  Watching till she wake.

"By the craggy hill-side,
  Through the mosses bare,
They have planted thorn-trees
  For pleasure here and there:
Is any man so daring
  As dig them up in spite,
He shall find their sharpest thorns
  In his bed at night.

"Up the airy mountain,
     Down the rushy glen,
We daren't go a-hunting
     For fear of little men:
Wee folk, good folk,
     Trooping all together,
Green jacket, red cap,
     And white owl's feather!"

In the lines:

"Down along the rocky shore
 Some make their home"

there is a reference to the fairy bridges—"a series of natural arches carved or shapen out of the cliffs in times long past by the rollers of the Atlantic," in the neighbourhood of Ballyshannon, while the Slieveleague headland is the only land lying between the fairy bridges and America. In "Happy England" there is a beautiful drawing, No. 79, by Mrs. Allingham (widow of the poet) of the fairy bridges with a distant view of Slieveleague. Mrs. Allingham, who is a member of the Royal Society of Painters in Water Colours, is the well-known water-colourist. She has, during a quarter of a century, produced nearly a thousand drawings, and, looked at from the point of view of her figures and her cottage subjects, she is of the same artistic school as Frederick Walker and Birket Foster.

The "Lepracaun" (Leprahaun), according to Dr. Hyde, is from the Irish "Leith Bhrogan," and so means the "Artisan of the Brogue"; according to other authorities (Joyce, etc.), the true etymology is luchor pan="little man." He is an industrious, canty, little sprite, who acts as shoemaker, cobbler, and tailor for the fairy gentry; and the country folk, especially in Donegal, will tell you that they sometimes see or hear these little creatures at their work under the hedge or in a dry ditch stitching and singing. The Lepracauns are elfs altogether peculiar to Ireland, and they have the secret of hidden gold. The peasants represent them as in appearance like tiny old men, who wear little cocked hats on the side of their heads, and have leather aprons hanging before them. If they take a fancy to a person they may, it is said, of their own free will guide him to a spot in the forth or rath where the gold is buried, and the country folk believe the fairy shoemaker may be forced to give you of his store of gold if you can only manage to keep your eye on him, but at the last moment, when you think you have caught him, he often manages to escape. In his poem, "The Lepracaun," Allingham represents a Donegal countryman pursuing this little sprite, and at last finding him, but the Lepracaun was too clever, and got off. Here is the last verse:

"I caught him at work one day myself,
    In the castle-ditch, where fox-glove grows,
A wrinkled, wizened, and bearded elf,
    Spectacles stuck on his pointed nose,
Leather apron, shoe in his lap—

        "Rip-rap, tip-tap,
            Tack-tack too!
        (A grasshopper on my cap!
            Away the moth flew!)
        Buskins for a fairy prince,
            Brogues for his son—
        Pay me well, pay me well
            When the job is done!"

"The rogue was mine beyond a doubt,
    I stared at him, he stared at me:
    'Servant, sir!' 'Humph!' says he,
And pulled a snuff-box out.
He took a long pinch, looked better pleased,
    The queer little Lepracaun
    Offer'd the box with a whimsical grace—
    Pouf! he flung the dust in my face,
And, while I sneezed,
    Was gone."

William Allingham, the celebrated Ulster
poet, was born in Ballyshannon, Co. Donegal, in
1824, and those who have visited that delightful
place will recollect the lines on the tablet on

the Bridge, which were left by the poet as an inscription to be placed on a stone which he wished his widow to put up to his memory near the River Erne he loved so well:

"Here once he roved, a happy boy,
  Along the winding banks of Erne;
And now, please God, with finer joy,
  A fairer world his eyes discern."

He was chiefly educated at what was, in his day, an exceptionally good classical school in his native town, and which was conducted by Mr. Robert Wray, M.A. (T.C.D.) At this school, just as happened at the same period in various parts of the North of Ireland, many pupils obtained an education which fitted them for the prominent positions which they afterwards filled with distinction and credit to themselves and to the nation. Allingham was for a short period a clerk in the Provincial Bank in Ballyshannon, of which his father was first manager, and at the present time the poet's brother occupies the same position. Not finding the routine of banking altogether congenial, he obtained another appointment in Her Majesty's (Victoria) Customs, and in this department he was for a time in Belfast, and also in Coleraine, but the greater part of his career in the Customs was spent in his native town, Ballyshannon, where he was controller. His official duties were light, and afforded him ample leisure to follow his literary pursuits. He was very much given to long walks and rides through the country, and was on the closest terms of friendship with the people, and he was a particular friend of children. It was during these rambles he picked up old ballads which he heard the Irish girls singing at their cottage doors, which he often altered, clothing them in a more perfect literary form. In the introduction to a most interesting book, "Letters of Dante Gabriel Rosetti to William Allingham," the editor, Dr. Birbeck Hill, says: "He could not get them (the ballads) sung till he got the Dublin 'Catnatch' of that day to print them on long slips of blue paper, like old songs, and if about the sea, with the old rough woodcut of a ship on the top. He either gave them away or they were sold in the neighbourhood. Then in his evening walks, he had at last the pleasure of hearing some of his own ballads sung at the cottage doors by the crooning lasses, who were quite unaware that it was the author who was passing by." In the "fifties" of the last century, he left his native district for London, and the rest of his life was spent in England. Retiring from the Government service in 1870, he became sub-editor of *Frazer's Magazine,* and four years later he succeeded Froude in the Editorial chair. He died in 1889. As evidence of the amount of his writings, an edition of his works published after his death comprises six volumes. His name and memory are ever green amongst the cottages of Donegal.

Another form of superstition still extant in some places in Ulster is the use of certain cures and charms for disease. In many country districts, if a person has erysipelas, it is customary to procure someone who has obtained a reputation for charming this disease away. It is astonishing how many people, otherwise intelligent, believe in the charming of erysipelas. In some places in Ulster, the moment a medical attendant pronounces a disease to be erysipelas, the friends advise that the charmer (often some one in the district) be brought. It is probable that the reason why this complaint is so often treated by charming is owing to the very old belief that erysipelas originates from fairy malice. I recollect, when a boy, seeing children with whooping cough passed by their parents three times under and over a donkey's body. Another cure for the same chronic complaint was to give to those affected two articles of food (*i.e.*, bread and milk, or bread and cheese), procured from two first cousins who were married. I remember well, when staying many years ago with relatives—first cousins who were married— seeing the country people in the neighbourhood come to the house and ask for two different kinds of food for their children, ill of this troublesome complaint. These charms for whooping cough are at present used in many parts of Ulster, and I may mention two other charms or cures still practised in our Irish northern province. If a child is afflicted with mumps, a donkey's bridle or winkers is put on his head, with the bit in his mouth. The child is then blindfolded with a handkerchief and led to a stream or well, of which he is made to drink three times in the name of the Trinity, the charmer at the same time repeating his incantation. He is then led back again, the bridle or winkers and handkerchief over his eyes are removed, and he is pronounced cured. For a severe headache, generally of a nervous type, the charmer performs what is called, "measuring the head," that is, he takes a variety of measurements vertically and longitudinally of the skull-cap, and then with his hands he compresses the head, saying at the same time it is "too open," and muttering certain prayers and charms. This process is repeated on several occasions, until at last the charmer pronounces the head "completely closed," on which the headache is said to disappear, and, fortunately for the sufferer, never to return again.

Again, one of my earliest recollections was, when staying at a house in County Down, hearing one of the principal servants request the owner of the house to order away from the premises an old beggar-woman who the country-folk said was possessed of the "evil eye," and had the power of bewitching the cows so that they would give no milk. In some parts of Ulster the superstition in reference to the "evil eye," which is of great antiquity in Ireland, still exists. It means that certain persons (men, and especially old women)—it is said those chiefly with dark, lowering eyebrows—are possessed of a certain gift from their birth, so that their glance or frown has a malignant influence when directed against either human beings or animals. Anything which is young, beautiful, or perfect of its kind, and which in consequence is admired, is liable to the ill luck which follows a glance of the "evil eye," and so, in some places, to avoid being thought to possess this influence, when looking at an infant or a young animal (as a foal), it is necessary at once to say, "God bless it." A person coming under the influence of the "evil eye" is declared to be "overlooked" by it (in the famous "casket" scene in "The Merchant of Venice," Portia says to Bassanio:

"Beshrew (? make evil or curse) your eyes
They have *o'erlooked* me, and divided me:
One half of me is yours, the other half yours—
Mine own, I would say; but if mine, then yours,
And so all yours"),

and in the case of an animal I have heard it said: "So and so," whom the country people thought had the "evil eye," "on a certain occasion 'blinkt' it," and as a result it did no good. The word "blink," or "elf-shot," as used in this sense in Ulster, means that by the influence of the "evil eye" the animal was injured. It is curious that in some parts of England "blink" means to turn beer or milk slightly sour, and the origin of the word has been sought in the glance of an "evil eye," the blinking of milk (souring or injuring it) being formerly ascribed to witchcraft. It is also said in some English counties at times of lightning storms, that the thunder "blinks" the milk. I knew a gentleman in County Antrim, who was very fond of horses, and he was suspected of having the "evil eye" influence, so that if he offered anyone a price for a horse, the belief of the country people was that it was better, as they put it, "to part with the animal to him, for if they didn't, the horse would go wrong in some way," in other words, they imagined this gentleman could, as they said, "blink" the horse, if he did not buy him.

In certain places a little thatch was taken off the roof of a house and burned under the nose of a horse that had been "blinkt," as this was supposed to be a way of charming the ill-effects that followed a "blink." "Thatch" is the old English thak; Dutch, dak; Swedish, tak. In "Henry V." Shakespeare writes:

"O, for honour of our land,
    Let us not hang like roping icicles
    Upon our houses *thatch,* whilst a more frosty
            people
    Sweat drops of gallant youth in our rich fields."

There is occasionally in a district of the country a person who is supposed to have this "evil eye" influence, and the country folk dislike meeting him if they are, say in the morning, going a journey. I have heard of cases where farmers going to the fairs with animals to sell would actually turn back if they met a man or woman with the "evil eye." Since I began to write this paper, one evening while hurrying to catch a train at a station in South Down, the driver of the car suddenly pointed out to me a little old woman in the road who, he said, was believed by the country people to have the "evil eye."

A medical friend told me that he knew a case in the neighbourhood of Ballymena, where a man suspected of the "evil eye" entered a farm house where they were churning in the kitchen. Those who saw him at once came to the conclusion that as the result of his presence there would be no butter, but as he gave a helping hand at the churn their fears were dispelled, because it is an omen that forebodes evil to pass a churn and not give a helping hand. The man, by giving the churn a "brash" (*i.e.,* a short turn of work or effort, probably of Scotch origin, but may be connected with the middle low-German "brasch"; or may be onomatopoeic, with associations with crash, dash, rash, splash) either did away with the influence of his own "evil eye" or the country people were wrong in thinking he had the "evil eye." In certain very superstitious districts if a young child takes ill, I have been told that someone is suspected, either out of malice or even ill-will, of having forgotten, when they saw the child, to say, "God bless it," or "God love it for a crater" (creature). Without being the least superstitious have we not all at times felt the unpleasant effect produced in a room where someone who has a bad expression in their eyes, or who looks in a furtive way, or, as it is said, "not straight at you," enters? Such people when they give evidence in a Court of Law carry little weight with the jury; but at other times they have an extraordinary influence, and so, what we call a magnetic or mesmeric effect or a bewitching influence, the uneducated or superstitious—if the influence is bad—say it is the "evil eye."

One often hears it said in country districts in Ulster that a person who can perform clever tricks by sleight of hand has the "black art." Originally the idea conveyed by this was that the remarkable feats of magic were done by means preternatural, derived from the prince of evil; or "black" may refer primarily to the dark and secret nature of the magician's art, but it is more probable that "black art" is a translation of the middle Latin ("Bog-Latin," as it is called) nigromantia, an apparent corruption, due to confusion with the Latin niger (black) of necromantia, a mediaeval Latin word derived from the Greek *nekromanteia* (*nekros*=a dead body, and *manteia*=divination, and so the modern necromancy) which meant originally divination, by calling up and conversing with the spirits of the dead. No doubt the common notion that the devil is black helped in confusing nigromantia for necromantia. We find references to the "Black art" in Marlow's "Faust," in Addison's "Spectator," and in the famous second scene of the first act of "The Rivals," where on Lydia Languish declining to promise to take a husband of her friend's choosing, Sir Anthony Absolute says to Mrs. Malaprop—"It is not to be wondered at ma'am; all this is the natural consequence of teaching girls to read. Had I a thousand daughters, by heaven! I'd as soon have them taught the *black art* as their alphabet!" So we see again the Ulsterman has good literary authority for his reference to the "black art."

The belief in omens is still very prevalent, and the people or things seen the first thing in the morning are considered to bring luck or the reverse. To meet a donkey and cart on the road early in the morning is a good omen, and if a black-avised (dark-complexioned) person calls the first thing on New Year's morning at any house he brings luck for the rest of that year to the house he visits. If a man, on entering a field, sees a hare cross his path it is very unlucky, and the sight of a weazel, or whitrit as it is called in Ulster, on the road under similar circumstances is not good. To find a four-leaved shamrock is lucky, or the shoe of a horse or donkey, which we so often see put over doors (the reference being to the manger where Christ lay). It is considered very unlucky to kill a robin redbreast, the reason for not injuring this little bird being that—according to a very prevalent tradition amongst the people— it plucked out of our Saviour's brow one of the sharpest thorns that pierced Him on the Cross, and in doing this its little breast was reddened with His blood. No one cares to kill a cricket, and I have often heard people say their noise at night in a house is sonsy or heartsome.

The reason why hares are considered unlucky is the curious belief that witches take their form to enter a field to do harm to the cattle.

It is a very common superstition that, if in going a journey you meet the magpie it is an ill omen, while any number, except one, brings luck, and hence the rhyme I remember since boyhood:

"One for sorrow,
 Two for mirth,
 Three for a wedding,
 Four for a birth,
 Five for silver,
 Six for gold,
 Seven for a secret that never may be told."

Some people don't like to begin work on a Friday, and the idea so prevalent that no one should remove to another house, or leave a situation on a Saturday, finds expression in the well-known Ulster saying:

"A Saturday's flit is a short sit."

In my boyhood it was common in County Armagh to hear the Christmas Rhymers near the close of the year. They came about in a sort of fancy dress, and after reciting or singing some verses outside, one, generally the smallest, was admitted, and holding his hat in one hand, and a brush or besom in the other, he said:

"Next come I, wee divil doit,
    Money I want, money I crave,
If ye don't give me money
    I'll sweep ye all to yer grave."

My friend and colleague at the Royal Victoria Hospital, Mr. J. A. Craig, F.R.C.S. (Eng.), has given me the following lines, which were formerly recited by the Christmas Rhymers in the Ballymoney district:

Omnes:

Room, room, brave gallant boys—
    Give us room to rhyme;
We have come to show our activity
    At this Christmas time.

Active youth and active age,
The like was never acted on a stage;
And if you don't believe what I say,
Enter in, St. George, and clear the way.

St. George:

Here comes I, St. George, from England have
    I sprung—
One of those noble deeds of valour to begin.
Seven long years in a close cave have I been
    kept,
And out of that into a prison leapt,
And out of that into a block of stone,
Where I made many a sad and grievous moan.
Many a giant did I subdue,
I ran the fiery dragon through and through—
I fought them all courageously,
And still will always fight for liberty.
Here I draw my bloody weapon:
Show me the man that dare me stand,
I'll cut him down with my courageous hand.

*A youth with blackened face here steps forward,
George says to him*:

"Who are you but a poor silly lad?"

The nigger replies:

"I am a Turkey champion, from Turkeyland I
    came,

To fight you, great George by name;
I'll cut you and slash you, and send you to
    Turkey
To make mince pies baked in an oven,
And after I've done I'll fight e'er a champion in
    Christendom."

*Here George sticks him with his sword. Having
done this he shouts*:

"A doctor, a doctor! Ten pounds for a doctor!
Is there never a doctor to be found who can
Cure this man of his deep and mortal wound?"

A doctor comes forward. He says:

"Here comes I, old Doctor Brown,
The best old doctor in the town:
I am a doctor pure and good,
And with my sword I'll staunch his blood.
If you've a mind his life to save
Full fifty guineas I must have."

George tests him. He says:

"What can you cure, Doctor?"

The Doctor:

"I can cure the plague within, the plague
    without,

The palsy or the gout.
Moreover than that," sez he
"If you bring me an old woman of threescore
　　and ten,
And the knuckle-bone of her toe be broken,
I can fix it again.
And if you don't believe what I say,
Enter St. Patrick and clear the way."

St. Patrick:

"Here comes I, St. Patrick, in shining armour
　　bright,
A famous champion and a worthy knight.
What was St. George?" sez he, "but St. Patrick's
　　boy,
Who fed his horse with oats and hay,
And afterwards he ran away."

This annoys St. George. They altercate:

G.—I say, by St. George, you lie, sir,
P.—Pull out your sword and try, sir.
G.—Pull out your purse and pay, sir.
P.—I'll run my sword through your body,
And make you run away, sir.

*In the middle of the squabble in comes Oliver
Cromwell.*

Oliver (loq.):

> "Here comes I, Oliver Cromwell, as you may
>   suppose,
> I've conquered many nations with my long
>   copper nose;
> I've made my foes to tremble and my enemies
>   for to quake,
> And I've beat my opposers till I've made their
>   hearts to ache;
> And if you don't believe what I say,
> Enter Beelzebub and clear the way."

Beelzebub:

> "Here comes I, Beelzebub,
> And over my shoulder I carry my club,
> And in my hand a dripping pan—
> I think myself a jolly old man;
> And if you don't believe what I say,
> Enter Divil Doubt and clear the way."

Divil Doubt:

> "Here comes I, wee Divil Doubt,
> If you don't give me money I'll sweep you all
>   out—
> Money I want, and money I crave,
> If you don't give me money I'll sweep you all to
>   your grave."

Omnes:

> "Ladies and Gentlemen,—Since our sport is
>   ended,
> Our box must now be recommended;
> Our box would speak if it had a tongue—
> Nine or ten shillings would do it no wrong.
> All silver, no brass; bad ha'pence won't pass."

Exeunt Omnes.

I am afraid this custom is now largely a thing of the past.

I wonder are the Ulster children of the present age as well acquainted as their parents were with Johnny Nod, who came towards bedtime, not from "the land of Nod, on the east of Eden," but right down the chimley (dialect form of chimney); are they told not to go out at "dayligone" (daylight going or gone=twilight) or duskiss (dusk) lest that awful person, "Raw Head and Bloody Bones" might catch them? Were they, during the late African war, frightened by the bogey, Paul Kruger, as their ancestors were in the early part of the last century by Bonaparte? Such was the dread inspired by that great warrior, that it permeated even the literature of the nursery, and children, as they heard a rhyme like this, delivered with adequate facial expression, were soon brought to reason:

"Baby, baby, naughty baby,
Stop your crying, child, I say,
Stop, or, I tell ye, Bonyparte 'ill pass this way,
And he'll bate you, bate you, bate you,
And he'll bate you into pap;
Gobble you, gobble you,
Snap, snap, snap!"

The word "gobble," used in this old nursery rhyme, is a frequentative of "gob," an abbreviation of the older "gobbet": a small piece or fragment, which is derived from the old French "gobbet" ("goubet," "gobet")=a morsel of food, which is in turn a diminutive of the old French "gob"=a gulp, and is ultimately of Celtic origin. "Gob" is used in two senses, first as meaning the mouth (we have also the dialect "gab" derived from the Gaelic "gob"=the beak or bill of a bird, the mouth, this is the Irish "gob," "gab," "cab"=the beak, snout, mouth, and with these may be compared the Welsh "gwp"=the head and neck of a bird. Hence, instead of saying, "hold your tongue," or "shut your mouth," the phrase in Ulster often is "shut up your gub" (another variant of "gob"). It is said by some that "gab" (derived from the old English "gabben")=to talk idly, is connected with the Celtic "gob" (a good talker has the "gift of the gab") and "give me none of yer (your) gab" (variants, "back-chat," "lip," "jaw"), heard sometimes in County Down and County Antrim, means, "give me no impudence." Probably "gabble" and "jabber" are connected with " gab." "Gab" is also used in the North of England and in Scotland as meaning the mouth, and hence the old proverb: "Ye take mair (more) in your gab than your cheeks can had" (hold), which has been modernised by our Transatlantic cousins into the well-known saying: "You have bitten off more tobacco than you can well chew." "Gob" has also a second meaning, which is a "mouthful." In Swift's "Lady's Journal" we find "gobble" used as follows:

> "The time too precious now to waste,
> And supper *gobbled* up in haste,
> Again afresh to cards they run."

The Ulsterman has a great affection and tender feeling for the dead, and in no way is this seen more than in his care of a grave. When the coffin is lowered to its last resting-place in the ground, and the grave is filled up with earth, soft mossy layers of sod or turf are placed on the top. These are called "scras" or "scraws," from the Irish and Gaelic word "scrath"=a turf; and although in "Drapier's Letters" Swift may write:
"Neither should that odious custom be allowed of cutting scraws (as they call them), which is flaying off the green surface of the ground, to cover their cabins or make up their ditches"; yet I am confident a true Ulsterman will always

reverence the word "scraw" from its association with the burial of his relatives or friends of the past.

A person who is buried is said to be "covered with the daisy sod" or the "daisy quilt," and so in "Denny's Daughter," Moira O'Neill writes:

> "She, the girl my own hands covered wi' the
> narrow *daisy quilt*,
> For the love of her,
> The love of her,
> That would not be my wife:
> Ay', the loss of her
> The loss of her,
> Has left me lone for life."

The same idea is conveyed in the common saying: "He's on the broad of his back, with his toes towards the daisies."

The Ulsterman's method of salutation when he meets an acquaintance on the road varies. He may say, "Good morrow," or "Morrow to you," or "Where are ye for?" or "The top o' the mornin'," as in the following lines from one of Moira O'Neill's "Songs of the Glens of Antrim":

> "I met an' ould caillach I knowed right well on
> the brow o' Carnashee;
> *The top o' the morning!* I says to her, 'God
> save ye!' she says to me";

or if he is very friendly, "Good morrow an' good luck," and the reply often is "Morrow to yourself." "Morrow" is apparently a corruption of "morning"—In Richard III., Shakespeare writes:

"Many good morrows to my noble lord"—

or he may say to a person he meets: "How are you?" or "How do you think you are?" and the reply may be short and laconic: "The very best," or "Rightly"; or he may salute in this way: "Is that yourself?" to which his friend may say: "It's all that's for me." There is no more common salutation in Ulster than "Is that you?" Suppose an examiner either of the Irish Intermediate Board or of Trinity College, or of the Royal University asked a candidate to analyse this very common Ulster method of greeting, "Is that you?" the candidate, if he is of a metaphysical turn of mind, might say: "*Subjectively*, it could only mean the person addressed, that is, myself; while *objectively*, and especially if the question was put suddenly on a dark night, or through a telephone, the querist might be in doubt whether he was the person addressed or somebody else. The reply to the question would clear up the difficulty."

Again the salutation may be: "You are wearing well," or "You are doing well on it," especially if the person addressed has recovered from a severe illness; or "How're ye doin'?" When an old person is asked how he is, he may reply: "I'm just putting in my wee bit time." Another odd method of salutation is: "It's new-ones to meet you," or "It's a sight for sore eyes to see you," the meaning conveyed being that the person addressed has been slow in calling. "You're not a day older since I seen ye last" is a complimentary salutation, as well as "Take care of yourself, for good people are getting scarce." When one Ulsterman, meeting another, says: "That's a fine growin' day," he may not speak accurately, but how better can he convey his meaning? and, if there is rain, he may add: "It's a fine day for young ducks."

A person who has lost flesh rapidly may, on being asked how he is, reply, "Badly; don't you see I'm all away to scrapin's (scrapings)"; or it may be said of him: "He's lavin' his clothes," or "He's hadden (holden) the-gether (together) by the help of the clathes" (clothes). On enquiring once from a countryman how an old clergyman in his neighbourhood was, he replied most graphically, "The Dane's getting short in his steps." This is part of the proverb: "He's getting long in the teeth and short in the steps," so characteristic of old age.

The terms used in the northern province to describe the qualities and appearance of men and women are most expressive, and many of them have almost become proverbs. A "fine bouncin' " or "strapping girl" is to be admired, as well as a "brave (very) smart one"; but the daughter of a respected mother is a "chip off a good block," and so more commendable. If she possesses monetary charms she is styled a "great catch," but in this case she must be all the more careful lest someone "should marry her money and only ask herself to the wedding," and if she makes a mistake in her marriage she will "tie a knot with her tongue which her teeth won't loose." A dirty woman is styled a "clart" (this is clearly taken from the Scotch "clarty," meaning dirty). The word "beclart"=to soil or dirty, dates back to the thirteenth century. In Burns' poem: "On being appointed to the Excise" we find it as follows:

"Searching auld wives' barrels,
Och, hon! the day!
That *clarty* barm should stain my laurels";

and if untidy, she may be said to have her hair like a "peas' wisp" (wisp: a bundle or bunch, is found in Henry VI., where Shakespeare writes:

"A *wisp* of straw were worth a thousand crowns
To make this shameless callet know herself").

Anyone who has seen growing peas will recognise the apt comparison of a wisp of them to untidy hair in a woman. If she is well dressed she is "cruel gran' " (very grand); but her beauty may be so apparent that fine garments do not matter, as "a bonny face becomes the dish-clout." Nature may have lavished on her such gifts of manner that she "could charm the birds off the bush," but she must not "set her cap" at anyone, and if she carries her head too loftily, she may be styled "a high-flyer."

There is a shrewd warning conveyed to mothers in the sayings: "Active mothers make leaden-heeled daughters," and "A soople (supple) mother mak's a sweer (a very old word=lazy) wean and a dawdlin' woman." It is too often the case that handsome children when they grow up lose their early beauty; how much better this is expressed in Ulster by the phrase: "Bonnie weans make ornary (ordinary) folk." A man who has not an assured means of livelihood is said to be "cooling and supping"; but if he has made his pile, and has retired, he is "living private"; if he has been long in a locality, as well as his fathers before him, he is styled an "ould residenter "; if he is an oddity he is styled "an ould 'curosity' " (curiosity); if he is smart "he has his wits about him." A man who unfairly reveals a secret on another is said to "discover" on him; a similar individual among boys at school is a "clash-bag"; if averse to change he is "an old fogey" (this odd word may be associated with the Swedish "fodge"=one in charge of a garrison, or it may be mediaeval Latin: vocatus for advocatus=patron or protector. Thackeray, in his amusing "Book of Snobs" has made the word classical when he writes: "Old Livermore, old Soy, old Chutney, the East Indian director; old Cutler, the surgeon, etc., that society of *old fogies* in fine, who give each other dinners round and round, and dine for the mere purpose of guttling—these again are dinner-giving snobs").

When you speak to an Ulsterman who is somewhat deaf, or, as he puts it, "a little hard-a-hearing," he may remark, holding his hand behind one of his ears like a trumpet, "I didn't catch what you said." The use of the word "catch," meaning to hear, or by an effort to seize by the senses (ear, eye) or intellect, is very common in the northern province. In "The Vicar of Wakefield" Goldsmith uses it: "Listening to catch the glorious sounds." It has also been used in this sense by Jowett in his "Plato," by Whewell, and by Hazlitt.

If he is puzzling himself to recall something, he tells you he is "cudgelling his brains" to recollect it. Although prepared at times, in true Hibernian fashion, to hit with his cudgel or stick any head that may appear, he uses this expression in reference to himself in a purely figurative sense; and he is prepared, if necessary, in defence of a friend, to "take up the cudgels," that is, to engage in a vigorous contest on behalf of one who, he thinks, has been wronged. According to some authorities, "cudgel" is derived from the old English kuggel, which is again of Celtic origin; the Welsh is coggl=a club; the Gallic is cuaille; the Irish is cuaill. Others say it is the early English cycgel—kucgel, the old Teutonic kuggelo—the original "y" having become "u", as in blush, clutch, and it is said not to be known in cognate languages. Cudgel is a fine old word, and in employing it in the saying "cudgelling his brains," the Ulsterman has the best of literary authority. In the famous churchyard scene in "Hamlet." when one of the clowns asks: "Who builds stronger than a mason, a shipwright, or a carpenter?" the other replies: *"Cudgel thy brains* no more about it, for your dull ass will not mend his pace with beating, and when you are asked this question next, say a grave-maker, the houses that he makes last till doomsday." The phrase has also been used by De Quincey and by Thackeray in "Pendennis." The saying to "take up the cudgels" dates back to the middle of the seventeenth century.

An "ignorant" fellow in Ulster is not one who is destitute of knowledge, rather the idea conveyed is that he is presuming, interfering, and one who does not know his proper position. The following story will illustrate the true Ulster use of the word:

At a railway station in County Derry a man, slightly under the influence of drink, who had seen better days, came up to speak to a former acquaintance who was sitting in a first-class railway carriage. As they were conversing, a boon companion walked up and presumed to join in the conversation, when his friend on the platform said, addressing him with the greatest contempt:

"Sir, you are grossly ignorant!"

When it is impossible to make a stupid person understand something he is asking about, the Ulsterman says: "I can't insense it into him." The word "eternal" is often employed as simply conveying great emphasis. An "eternally" wet day is one that is more wet than usual. At the Belfast Assizes, recently, in a case in which a woman brought an action against a railway company for damage done through their negligence, the leading K.C. for the defence, in cross-examining the woman's husband, asked: "Her nerves are not so bad as they were, are they?" to which the man replied: "Well, if my explanation goes for anything I would say she is *eternally destroyed*." Great laughter followed, and the K.C. remarked: "Oh! well, I wouldn't say that. I don't think any railway company could do it. The damages would be such that I don't know where we would be if that went on." Now the Ulsterman did not mean to convey what, owing to its being wrongly understood, occasioned such amusement in Court, that his wife was destroyed both as regards the present and the future world. All he desired to imply—in as emphatic Ulster phraseology as he could employ—was that his wife was very badly injured, and that she would never be the same physically again.

Another word used in the same sense—"extremely" is "mortal" or "mortyal"—*i.e.,* "It's a mortyal pity of him" (said of a person who has had a trial), or "It's a mortal wet day." In "Corrymeela," by Moira O'Neill, the Antrim man living in England, says:

"D'ye mind me now, the song at night is *mortial* hard to raise,
The girls are heavy goin' here, the boys are ill to plase;
When one'st I'm out this workin' hive, 'tis I'll be back again,
Ay, Corrymeela, in the same soft rain."

In "Oliver Twist" Dickens writes: "Forty-two *mortal* long hard-working days." "Cruel," is another of the same type of terms used to convey emphasis: "We had very few 'crul' (cruel) fine days this summer." In the epilogue to "Two Noble Kinsmen," by Fletcher (and another), we find: "I'm cruel fearful"; while in his Diary, under the date July 31st, 1662, the immortal Pepys notes: "Met Captain Brown of the Rosebush, at which he was *cruel* angry." When Ulster folk meet, they, like others, sometimes talk of their troubles. One who has suffered greatly will say: "Misfortunes never come single"; another of a humorous turn will add: "Misfortunes make strange bedfellows"; while a third, of the Mark Tapley type, will take pleasure in pointing out that there are sure to be more trials in store. Irritated by such pessimism, another of the group—this time, an optimist—will say: "It's a long lane that has no turn," or "Don't cross the bridge until you come to it," or "It's time enough to bid the old fellow good-morrow when you meet him." As is well-known, in Ireland at present a keen contest is raging between the wretchedly underpaid and far-too-overworked dispensary doctors and the boards of guardians. The question came before the Newry Board recently, when the clerk said that the guardians had had no trouble with the medical officers in the Newry Union. One of the guardians, evidently of a poetical and militant type, replied: "But we do not know when we might have, and it is too late to sharpen the sword when the drum beats for battle," and was immediately answered by a wittier and more practical colleague: "It's time enough to bid the old fellow good morrow when we meet him."

When an Ulsterman wishes to pay his wife a great compliment, he says: "She's my best rib." This saying has reference to a common belief that since the days of Eve men have one rib less than women; and so if a man's wife is in every respect suitable, he calls her his "best rib," or "She's just my own hand's morrow" (that is, what the left hand or left eye is to the right=its morrow or mate), while, in return, how better can she show her respect for her husband than by styling him "Himself," or "Him," and so, to emphasize a statement in total disregard of Lindley Murray, she avers: "Himself says it, and so it be to be true." In the "Sea Wrack," Moira O'Neill writes:

> "The wrack was dark an' shiny where it floated
>   in the sea,
> There was no one in the brown boat but only
>   him an' me:
> *Him* to cut the sea wrack, me to mind the boat,
> An' not a word between us the hours we were
>   afloat.
>   The wet wrack,
>   The sea wrack,
> The wrack was strong to cut."

An old and much-valued servant on being told by her mistress that a grandson had just arrived, asked: "Is it like himself?" What she meant to convey was really was the child like its father. When an ill-matched pair are constantly quarrelling, the neighbours say: "They are as contrary as the tongs tied thegether (together), and aye (always) chappin'," or "They're like sweeled (tied by a strap) goats, aye on the opposite sides of the ditch." The word "sweeled" is also used with the meaning, swathed or wrapped or rolled round, as an infant is said to be "sweeled" with a roller, and the piece of leather rolled round the top of a whip is said to be "sweeled." A bold jade is styled a "regular heeler" (a heeler being a gamecock that strikes out with its spurs, or one who catches up by the heels, that is, who undermines or supplants.) Of an ignorant fellow it is remarked: "He doesn't know B from a bull's foot"; while of a talkative fool people say: "He'll never drown; he's only a blether" (bladder). How expressive the phrases: "Eaten bread is soon forgotten," "He was cut out for a gentleman, but the devil ran away with the patthurn" (pattern), "Listeners rarely hear well of themselves," "He's no chicken for all his cheepin'," "It's too late to close the stable door when the steed's gone," "A wink's as good as a nod to a blind horse," "Don't look a gift horse in the mouth."

A silly person is said to "have a slate off," or "want's a square of being round," or "is not all there"; while of a constant talker some one may allege "He'd talk the horns off a moily cow," or "He'd talk a dog blind." Of a man who pretends to be younger than he really is, someone may say: "He's many a nick on his horn." When a family of low origin take on airs, the Ulsterman, to indicate that they are merely upstarts, will say: "No banshee'll skirl when they're stark," a curious example of the use of old English, Scotch, and Irish words, and throwing an interesting and suggestive light on the origin of the Ulster race. Banshee is purely native Irish, being a phonetic spelling of Bean-sidhe=woman of the fairies=old Irish, ben-side. Skirl is the unassibilated form of the Scotch shirl, which is a transposition of shrill; while stark is derived from the old English stark, the Anglo-Saxon stearc, the Danish sterk, the low German sterk, and the Icelandic sterkr. No saying could so well convey the meaning; the banshee being the apparition or guardian who, by its appearance and wail, foretells the death of the chief of an old Irish noble family. In Allingham's "The Banshee" we read:

> "Heard'st thou over the fortress wild geese flying and crying?
> Was it a grey wolf's howl? wind in the forest sighing?
> Wail from the sea, as of wreck? Hast heard it, comrade? Not so!
> Here all's still as the grave, above, around, and below.

> "The cry, the dreadful cry! I know it—louder and nearer.
> Circling our Dun—*the banshee*, my heart is frozen to hear her!
> Saw you not in the darkness a spectral glimmer of white
> Flitting away? I saw it!—evil her message to-night!

> "Constant, but never welcome, she to the line of our chief,

Bodeful, baleful, fateful, voice of terror and
>grief.
Dimly burneth the lamp—hush! Again that
>horrible cry!
If a thousand lives could save thee, Tierna,
>thou shouldest not die!

"Now! what whisper ye, clansmen? I wake. Be
>your words of me?
Wherefore gaze on each other? I, too, have
>heard the banshee:
Death is her message; but ye, be silent. Death
>comes to no man
Sweet as to him who in fighting crushes his
>country's foeman."

It is well if anyone has sustained an injustice
to blame the real culprit, that is, "to put the saddle
on the right horse"; and when several people are
equally blameworthy they must all take their
chance of being punished, in other words: "Every
herring must hang by its own head," an allusion
to the iron rod one often sees outside little shops,
which carries a number of herrings, through the
heads of which it is pierced.

If a man has lost his wife he is a "wida-man";
a great talker is "a fine level-cracking fellow" (the
word "crack" with the meaning to talk freely is
used all over Ulster. It is a very old word, and we
have it in Pilgrim's "Sea-Voyage":

" 'What, howe, mate! thou stondyst to ny,
Thy felow may not hale the by;
Thus they begyn to *crake*."

It has an entirely different meaning in other parts of the United Kingdom, that is, to boast or brag, and Burton, in his "Anatomy of Melancholy," uses it in this sense: "Galen *cracks* how many several cures he hath performed in this kind by use of baths alone."

The word "crack" is also used in Ulster as indicating a very short space of time—*i.e.*, "It won't be a *crack* till I'm there." "In a jiffy" means the same, and is often heard in Antrim and Down. Curiously, it is found in "Ingoldsby Legends," as follows:

" 'And oh!' he exclaimed, 'let them go catch my
skiff:
I'll be home in a twinkling and back in a jiffy.' "

A vulgar person is said to be "as coarse as bane (bean) straw"; while if he exhibits signs of peevishness, the people declare he is "as lumpy as pritty-oaten" (*i.e.*, bread made of oatmeal and potatoes).

If a man is not specially courageous he is "afeard of his own shada" (shadow); if he is selfish, he "wouldn't put his heel where his toe is to oblige his neighbour"; if his attendance at church is not regular the people say: "He's not like his forebears—he's no gospel greedy"; if in appearance he is short and stout, he is styled: "A wee butt of a man," or "He's just as broad as he's long"; if he walks as if lame, he is "hirplin" (this is of Scotch origin). Burns, in the "Holy Fair," says: "The hares were *hirplin* down the furs"; and in Dr. John Brown's "Spare Hours" we have the word as follows: "His aged grandmother was wont to *hirple* out to the Lindsaylands Road to meet him on his way home." If he does things the wrong way "He always puts the cart before the horse"; if a man is thrifty, people say of him: "He ploughs both the head and the foot rig"; if he looks after his own interests, "He knows on what side his bread is buttered"; if he always takes good care of himself, "He swims near the broo" (bank)—broo is a dialectal variant of brow. A man who stops at nothing would "Steal the cross off a donkey"; if a man usually easy to work with shows signs of irritability in the morning, it is said, "He has got out at the wrong side of the bed the day," or a friend may say of him in such circumstances, "I doubt the wind's in the aist" (east); or a man may be "as crookid as the hind leg of a dog," or "as cross as a bag of weasels," or "as hungry as a grew" (greyhound), "as full as a fiddler," "as sober as a judge," "as yellow as a duck's fut" (foot), "as busy as a nailer," "as blunt as a beetle," or "like a hen on a hot griddle" (fussy and fidgetty), or as "thrawn as a corkscrew," or "as thrawn as a hay rope," or "he's as deep as a draw well," or "slippery as an eel," or he may "tell lies faster than a dog can trot," or "he may not be so saft (soft) as he lets on" (pretends). Of a man slow in paying for anything he has purchased, it is said: "He keeps time between him and the day"; he does not follow the advice contained in the proverb: "Short reckonings make long friends." A "Luck penny" is the small sum of money given back for luck by the seller to the payer, its amount depending on the size of the transaction and the "cleverness" (generosity) of the seller.

Of a woman it may be said, if she is constantly complaining, and who thinks herself worse than she really is: "Och! she's like a layin' hen, more onaisy than sick"; while, if she boasts of her work, people say: "Her eggs are not worth all her cackling," or "It's not the hen cackles the most lays the biggest eggs." A woman no one can trust, and who is always at some mischief, is compared to a troublesome cow: "If she doesn't kick she will chaw claes" (clothes). A car-driver at Rostrevor said recently, when pointing out a very rich lady to the person he was driving: "She's a millionaire, or what is the female for that."

When a man makes great boasting of what he is going to do, but in the end accomplishes little, the Ulsterman says: "Great cry and little wool, as the de'il said when he pluckt the pig."

Of a person currying favour in expectation of a benefit, a neighbour will remark: "There's a great *bigness* between the cow and the haystack." "Bigness" in this sense means friendship or intimacy. The word "great" is used in the same way, hence it is said of two people: "They're very great" (intimate), as well as the word "thick," and hence the well-known saying: "They are as thick as thieves," which rather conveys the idea that the reason for their friendship is not a worthy one. When a person has failed in something, a looker-on remarks: "You missed that, as you missed your mother's blessing." To indicate that a man cannot have success in life without its accompanying trials, it is said: "A car does not go fast that is not jaupped" (dirtied). In Ardglass and Kilkeel, where many of the poorer classes live by fishing, they say of a lazy fellow who does not take advantage of his opportunity: "The mouth of his net is behind the tail of the herrings" (the fish get through before he is ready).

When a man has not the stability to follow one course of action in life, it is said of him: "A rolling stone gathers no moss." The proverb must be a very old one, as in Wyatt's "How to use the Court" we find

"And on the stone that still doth turn about
There groweth no mosse."

A friend of mine living in Western Canada told me he quoted this saying—"A rolling stone gathers no moss"—to a stranger who, in coming to that colony, said to him that he had been in every State in North America, but had not "struck oil" yet; when, in return, the wanderer (who was originally a County Down man) replied: "A sitting hen never grows fat."

Again, a man may be "as narrow as the rim of a sixpence," "as hard as a whinstone," or "as awkward as a plough upstairs," or so innocent-looking that "you would think butter wouldn't melt in his mouth," or he may be "too sweet to be wholesome," or as "innocent looking as a pet fox"; or he may be one of those undesirable men who give you a "back-spang" that is, fair to your face but treacherous behind your back (the word spang=a violent blow, a variant of spank, is met with in provincial English and Scotch, but in its Ulster use it conveys the idea of want of straightness or treachery). Of a man who cannot be trusted, it is said: "You couldn't trust him farther than you could see him," or "He's a bad plant," or "He has a bad drop in him," or "He has a kick in his gallop"; and if his progenitors have not borne a good reputation, it will be said: "What's bred in the bone stays long in the flesh," and some one may prophecy of him: "That boy'll dance on nothing yet" (be hanged), or "Hemp's sown for him" (in reference to the hangman's noose).

When a man is a hard worker people say you would "need to rise early to catch him"; and if he has a good appetite his friends need not be uneasy, although he complains about the state of his health, for "An atin' horse rarely founders," and "The hungry eye sees far." He may, however, through stress of circumstances, become "As poor as a church mouse," and those who know him well may say: "He hasn't what would jingle on a tombstone," or "He has neither money, marvels (marbles), nor chalk to make a ring," or "He has *four* outs and *one* in":

> "*Out* of money, *out* of clothes,
> *Out* at the heels, and *out* at the toes,
> But *in* debt."

And, finally, he may be compelled "To take the benefit of the Act" (Bankruptcy Court), or "Make a moonlight flit." A man on the contrary who is thrifty, and has saved something, is said "To have something by him for a rainy day." If the country people believe a man who has "failed" possesses means, they say: "He has closed with a full hand," that is, he could pay twenty shillings in the £.

Of a man who makes a great "stir" in a district, and by his unusual success draws attention to himself, people say: "Every dog has his day," and if, after having gone up as a rocket he comes down like a stick, but not in the way the people prophesied, it will be remarked: "There's many a way of killing a dog besides choking him with butter."

A person who engages in a bad speculation "has got a footless stocking without a leg." His relatives may give him financial assistance, whereupon the neighbours will say: "They're only making a coffin for a dead horse" (that is, "Throwing good money after bad"). In speaking once to an Ulsterman in reference to a friend recently deceased, who left a large family, I ventured to remark that I was glad to hear he was insured. He replied, very drily: "Ay, but that's a dead horse" (he meant to convey he was in debt). A man may notice a neighbour so slightly that he say s of him: "He hasn't a word to throw to a dog." If he is not hospitable to a caller, the caller will say: "He never asked me had I a mouth on me." When he speaks his remarks may be pointless or even vulgar, and so someone says: "What would you expect from a pig but a grunt?" or "Give him a fool's pardon," or "Do you think I would even my wit to him?" A man well dressed has his "Sunday Shute" on, and so Drennan writes:

> "Were I linkin' in heaven,
> With yon Pleiades seven,
> All shaven and shriven,
> In my *Sunday shute* clane
> I would give them the slip,

And to Newcastle dip,
To walk with bare feet,
Tollybranaghan Lane."

"He could not hit a flying turf-stack," is said of a person who is a bad shot. When an Ulsterman sees something painful or unpleasant to him, he says to his neighbour: "I hope I'll never see the likes of it again," and the friend addressed will reply: "Ay, and keep your eyesight." If one has no respect for the feelings of another he "rides roughshod over him," and the person aggrieved may say of him: "He'll never sole-leather me again." A person in talking to one he meets may, by some remark, "affront" him (Milton in "Paradise Lost" uses it in this sense of offend:

"Only our foe,
Tempting, *affronts* us with his foul esteem
Of our integrity");

and as an indication, he will remark as a result: "I seen a cloud pass over his countenance." A coachman of a lady who was accustomed to drive fast horses, by a mistake on one occasion put a slow animal in a machine for his mistress. On emerging from her house she suddenly observed the horse, and her general disgust with the situation was afterwards graphically described by the coachman, an Ulsterman: "She wouldn't have been worse *affronted* if you had handed her a pross" (process=summons).

A baby is "cut for the pox," and when it is able to walk alone it is "fit to travel"; if it has no shoes it is "barefut." The Glensman in Moira O'Neill's "Corrymeela" writes:

> "The people that's in England is richer nor the
>   Jews
> There's not the smallest gossoon but *thravels*
>   in his shoes!
> I'd give the pipe between me teeth to see a
>   *barefut* child,
> Och! Corrymeela an' the low south wind";

it may "fluster" (flooster) about its mother (flooster=to flatter or wheedle, is, I think, purely Ulster); if a child is spoiled it is "petted on" (from the Irish peat=a pet) its mother; and if precocious, it is "ould-fashioned." At school, a boy playing at marbles likes a good "taw" (the origin of this word is unknown, but Cowper, in "Tirocinium," speaks of

> "The little ones . . . .
> As happy as we once, to kneel and draw
> The chalky ring, and knuckle down at *taw*")

to shoot from "trig." Most Ulster children know what "bitin' billy" and "yellow-man" taste like. A boy with his "galluses" (suspenders) broken, and no "whang" in his boot (a variant of thwang, now thong) is very untidy.

An Ulster girl at school writes home she is "thinking long," meaning that she is longing for her home and relatives. It is a most expressive saying, and is beautifully conveyed in Moira O'Neill's

A SONG OF GLENANN.

"Och! when we lived in ould Glenann
    Meself could lift a song!
An' ne'er an hour by day or dark
    Would I be *thinkin' long.*

"The weary wind might take the roof,
    The rain might lay the corn;
We'd up an' look for betther luck
    About the morrow's morn.

"But since we come away from there
    An' far across the say,
I still have wrought, an' still have thought
    The way I'm doin' the day.

"An' now we're quarely betther fixed,
    In troth! there's nothing wrong:
But me and mine, by rain an' shine
    We do be *thinkin' long.*

This phrase by some has been regarded as an Ulster vulgarism to be corrected, but those conversant with "Romeo and Juliet" will recollect how, in the tragic scene where Juliet is found dead, Paris exclaims:

"Have I *thought long* to see this morning's face,
And doth it give me such a sight as this?"

As illustrating some points in the folk-lore of Ulster, I have quoted freely from the writings of Moira O'Neill and William Allingham. Their songs and lyrics are creative, full of imagination and humour, and of sympathy with the Ulster character and temperament. Moira O'Neill has more of what I have spoken of as the Celtic note, and in her songs we find the very expressions and peculiar sayings used everyday by the people. Allingham has a great love for nature and for children, and perhaps shows more liking for fairy lore, but he clothes his lyrics in ordinary phraseology; in this respect having probably been influenced by his friendship with Tennyson and Carlyle, Rosetti, Ruskin, and Millais. Up to the present, Moira O'Neill is best known in literature by her songs; Allingham has written many other articles in addition to his charming lyrics. Moira O'Neill may be regarded as the Burns, Allingham as the Coleridge or Scott of Ulster.

If a person is not easily affected by criticism,

people say: "It just went off him like water off a duck's back"; and if a man leaves a number of people who are discussing some subject in which he has exhibited little interest, some one may say: "Oh, he has other fish to fry." The most important person in a large connection of people is "the top of kin." "Far-out friends" are usually recognized if successful in life, otherwise they are to be considered as "poor relations."

The phrases and expressions one constantly hears in Ulster indicate how observant the people are who employ them. They have endless forms of sayings to describe the varied appearance of the face. A person whose face is covered with pock-marks is said to be "pock-arr'd" (arr is an old word found in Danish ar, Swedish arr, and Icelandic orr, meaning a scar). A person with a hare-lip, is "hare-scart" (hare scarred). One who talks through a cleft palate is said to "sneevle" (an obsolete form of snivel). One (generally applied to a woman) whose upper lip is expressionless from the absence of the usual depression in the centre below the level of the nose is said to have no "trinket to her lip." ("Trinket" is an essentially Ulster word applied to the water-course by the roadside. It apparently is for trinklet, and is derived from trinkle and -et, a variant of tricklet,=a small trickling stream.)

And the hands and feet readily lend themselves to comment. A man with no responsibilities is said "to have a free foot and a fellah (fellow) for it." "Something done among hands," means something outside the ordinary work. A place may be "near hand a mile" from a town. Twenty "hands" may be working in a field, and some may be so awkward that they have "no hands at all"; and a smart man at work may, if his fellow-workers are not "coming much speed" be asked to "put his hand till" and hurry on the job. A very busy person is said to "have his hands full." A person who blunders "puts his foot into it," and when he has made an utter mess of things it may be said: "He has put his foot into it up to the elbow." On the other hand a man may show good sense by "putting his right foot foremost," and some people are so lucky that they always "fall on their feet"; and a "footy" man is very contemptible, and if obstinate he won't "budge a foot." The word "hannel" (handle) means to hurry, and the following story will indicate the way it is used. As I was once driving from the station of a country town in Ulster on a car we met another vehicle approaching the railway station, on which there was an old lady as the only passenger. As we passed, the driver said to my Jehu: "Will I hit her?" to which he replied: "Ay, if you *hannel*." When the first driver said, waving his whip, "Will I hit her?" he had no idea of striking his old lady passenger with his whip; he meant could he "hit" (catch) the train; and when my carman said: "Ay, if ye hannel," he meant, yes, if he hurried on. Speaking of the train, instead of saying: "Is this the place where they collect the tickets?" the Ulsterman puts it: "Is it here they *lift* the tickets?" To take a "wee dander" (daunder, dauner) means to go an aimless walk, hence one person says to another: "Will you come for a dander?" It is connected with the Scotch "dandill"=to go about idly and "dandle." I have come across the word in Mrs. Carlyle's "Letters," and in Barrie's "Window in Thrums." It has nothing to do with the saying: "To get one's dander up" (this word is said to be a corruption of dandruff, and conveys the idea of rubbing one's hair the wrong way, and so getting one into a passion). It is used by Thackeray in "Pendennis," and by Lowell in "The Biglow Papers." Dander is closely related to "saunter" (old French, s'aventurer), to walk in a listless, leisurely way. A literary friend of mine was once staying at Hughenden, when another guest asked the host if he walked much, to which Dizzy replied: "I never walk? I only saunter." A common saying, indicating a large number or a great quantity, is a "power"—*i.e.*, a countryman will say of a meeting, that there was "a power" at it, or of a farmer that he has "a power" of sheep. It is simply power or force as estimated by numbers, and so is analogous with the word "strength," as the strength of a regiment (in "All's Well that Ends Well," Shakespeare writes: "Demand of him of what strength they are a-foot"), and has nothing to do with another similarly pronounced well-known Ulster phrase: "A pour of rain," which is simply a downpour. Some people on hearing an Ulsterman say of a friend that he had "a power" of money, might think the phrase vulgar, but it has been rendered classical by Richardson in "Pamela" as follows: "I am providing *a power* of pretty things for her against I see her next."

The word "heap" is used in the same way, we find it in Moira O'Neill's "Forgettin' ":

"Och, never fear, my jewel!
     I'd forget ye now this minute,
If I only had a notion
     O' the way I should begin it;
But first an' last it isn't known,
     The *heap* o' throuble's in it.

"Meself began the night ye went,
     An' haven't done it yet;
I'm nearly fit to give it up,
     For where's the use to fret?
An' the memory's fairly spoilt on me
     Wid' mindin' to forget."

Certain names, sayings, and proverbs have come to be associated with particular places in Ulster.

Everyone knows "Kitty of Coleraine," immortalised in the famous Irish song:

"As beautiful Kitty one morning was tripping
  With a pitcher of milk for the fair of
    Coleraine,
When she saw me she stumbled, the pitcher
    down tumbled,
  And all the sweet buttermilk watered the
    plain.
'Oh, what shall I do now? 'Twas looking at you
    now!
  I'm sure such a pitcher I'll ne'er see again.
'Twas the pride of my dairy. Oh, Barney
    McCleary,
  Your sent as a plague to the girls of
    Coleraine.'

"I sat down beside her, and gently did chide
    her,
  That such a misfortune should give her
    such pain;
A kiss then I gave her, and before I did leave
    her,
  She vowed for such pleasure she'd break it
    again.
'Twas the haymaking season—I can't tell the
    reason—
  Misfortunes will never come single, 'tis
    plain!
For very soon after poor Kitty's disaster,
  The devil a pitcher was whole in Coleraine"

(It is an interesting fact that the authorship of these verses, so well known all over Ireland is, like that of "The Cruiskeen Lawn," "The Night before Larry was stretched," "Johnny, I hardly knew ye," "Brian O'Linn," and "Nell Flaherty's Drake," unknown); and "Peg of Limavady," celebrated by Thackeray in his "Irish Sketches":

> "Beauty is not rare
>> In the Land of Paddy
> Fair beyond compare
>> Is Peg of Limavady,

> "Citizen or squire,
>> Tory, Whig, or Radi-
> Cal would all desire
>> Peg of Limavady.

> "And till I expire,
>> Or till I grow mad, I
> Will sing unto my lyre
>> Peg of Limavady!"

And some may have heard of that lady called

"Isabella,"

who had

"A gingham umbrella,"

and was married to

"A sandy-whiskered fella,"

who lived

"Down below Portadown."

"Tanderagee no pinch," a well-known term when used of anything, means that there is no stint. It had its origin, it is said, at the time that town in County Armagh was at the zenith of its prosperity as a great flax market, and when there was "no pinch" or stint in the way whiskey was offered; on the other hand, "A Tanderagee way of talking," means, I am told, to be always on the grumble. Of a woman who is "knowing"—what our American friends term "cute"—it is said: "She could keep Omagh," an allusion to the gaol there. A town that is not increasing in size is said to be a "finished town." We have all heard of "Good old County Down," and "One shot more for the honour of Down," were the last words of a distinguished Comber man, Major-General Sir Robert Rollo Gillespie, K.C.B., as he fell shot through the heart before the fort of Kalunga, in the Himalayas, while commanding the Meerut division of the Bengal troops.

To "make a Ballyshannon of it," is a curious term, the meaning of which the following incident will explain: A keen "hard-fisted" Northerner was buying some articles in a shop in Belfast. The owner quoted them at one shilling each, the buyer offered sixpence each, and as neither seemed inclined to yield, a bystander said: "Make a Ballyshannon of it," that is, to use another Ulster expression, he advised "to split the differ," making the price ninepence, which was agreed upon. Those who have read Allingham's "Emigrant's Farewell" will remember

> "Adieu to Belashanny! where I was bred and
>   born;
> Go where I may, I'll think of you, as sure as
>   night and morn—
> The kindly spot, the friendly town, where every
>   one is known,
> And not a face in all the place but partly seems
>   my own;
> There's not a house or window, there's not a
>   field or hill,
> But, East or West, in foreign lands I'll recollect
>   them still
> I leave my warm heart with you, tho' my back
>   I'm forced to turn,
> So adieu to Belashanny, and the winding
>   banks of Erne!"

Ballyshannon is situated on each side of the Erne, so "to make a Ballyshannon" of anything, means to halve or divide it.

Lisburn is often spoken of as old Lisnagarvey, its original name. It was of Newry that Swift wrote his famous lines:

> "High church,
> Low steeple,
> Dirty streets,
> Proud people."

Everyone has heard of the famous "Book of Armagh," and tradition tells us that the bones of the Patron Saint of Ireland lie at Downpatrick, either within the Cathedral, or in the adjoining graveyard outside; but few, I believe, are aware that in former ages leper hospitals existed in both these old cities. Several years ago when investigating for my old and revered teacher, the great all-round specialist, Mr. Jonathan Hutchinson, the question of the existence in early times of leper institutions in Ireland, a piece of work that was so well done for Scotland by the late Sir J. Simpson, I came across this interesting fact. Part of the results of this research—in which I received the greatest assistance from the late Bishop Reeves— has been published in *The Polyclinic*.

Dr. Reeves enjoyed the reputation of being the most accurate Irish antiquarian of his time, and on one occasion, in discussing with him the much debated question of the relative antiquity of Armagh and Downpatrick, the erudite Bishop said he believed Armagh was the older of the two.

A man may be "as long as Cookstown" (that is, a very tall man—Cookstown being largely one long street), "as hard as Derry's walls," or "as slippy (slippery) as a Bann eel" (at Toomebridge), or he may be "deeper and dirtier than the Glenwherry bogs," or so deformed that people may say of him: "He's aye to one side like Clogher" (with its shops, etc., on one side of the street). Banagher has been immortalized in the saying: "That beats Banagher, and Banagher bangs the de'il." In County Derry, near Dungiven, there is the old church of Banagher, and adjacent to it a building called the Abbey or Monastery. It is said that O'Heney, a saint, was the founder of both, and his effigy exists on the western side of the Abbey. In the churchyard is situated the tomb of the saint, and the sand adjacent to it (as in the case of St. Patrick's grave in Downpatrick) is regarded as sacred. In a horse-race whoever can throw some of this Banagher sand on the rider as he passes, ensures success to his horse; hence at horse-races Banagher men were thought to be certain to win, as they possessed the lucky sand; if thrown over a house it protects the house from burning. This sand carries virtue with it wherever it goes, but it should, to prove efficacious, be lifted and given to anyone asking for it by a real descendant of the saint, and I am told there is only one person in the district (he lives at Dungiven) who can do so at present. The sand is often carried away by emigrants to ensure their success, especially in America, so Banagher brings luck and keeps off or "bangs the de'il," and anything that beats Banagher must be very remarkable in many ways.

When a place (I won't name the Ulster town to which I first heard it applied) is out of the way and hard to reach, and altogether uninteresting, it is said to be "at the back of beyant" (beyond), that is, it is even more distant than "beyant (beyond) the beyants," a phrase more expressive than "a God-forsaken spot," or the "back of God-speed." An old lady, many years deceased, who lived all her life in the neighbourhood of Belfast, used to remark: "It's out of the world and into Holywood."

A word or two in conclusion about the humour of Ulster. One sometimes hears visitors to Ireland say there is little wit or humour in the northern province, but this is due to a very superficial knowledge on their part of the people "North of the Boyne," where these peculiar features form a marked characteristic of the inhabitants. The humour of the North of Ireland differs from that of the South in not being so apparent and spontaneous, and it is not so topsy-turvy; it is of a drier kind, but at the same time can be as sparkling as that met with in any other part of the country. One feature about the northern humour is that while it is not so much on the surface, and in many cases not so evidently prepared beforehand as you find it in the south, it is not so readily exhausted. In driving through Dublin, the jarvey will at once, when you mount his vehicle, fire off some humorous saying; in the North of Ireland the carman, on the contrary, waits until you draw it out of him by some remark, but, while the carman in the south shows by the twinkle in his eye that he is amusing you, his northern confrere never exhibits by any emotional evidence that he is poking fun at you. A few examples will illustrate the northern humour:

1.—A clergyman, who for many years preached in Ulster, was celebrated for a very ornate and rhetorical style. On one occasion being asked to lecture to a country audience in the centre of County Antrim, he selected as his subject "Savonarola." After the lecture (a very florid one), on going out of the church where the address was delivered, he and his host (the local clergyman) met a well-known member of the congregation who had been present. "What did you think of the lecture?" said the local cleric. The lay friend at first, as is so often the habit in the North, said nothing, but on the lecturer himself repeating the same question, he replied: "It was a gran' discourse, but I am thinking sir, it needed a heap o' spellin' " (spelling).

2.—One day, as I was driving in County Down from a station to meet a medical friend, I remarked to the driver of the hack car that his horse was making a good deal of noise; this he altogether questioned at first, but as we reached the top of a steep hill the "roaring" became so evident that I again drew his attention to it, when, without a smile, he made the extraordinary reply: "Oh, sir, it's the rubber tyres you heerd" (heard)— the wheels of the car were rubber tyred. I replied I had never heard them so loud before, when he rejoined: "I mane, sir, if there were no tyres on the wheels, you wouldn't hear the ould mare."

3.—On another occasion I told the carman he had only fifteen minutes to accomplish the journey to a country station. He said it was too little, and, on my urging in reply, that another carman at the same station (a rival of his) had told me he could "cover the distance" in ten minutes, he drily remarked: "Oh, he has a quare imagination, and you know, sir, imagination is a great help to a doctor's medicine."

4.—It used to be common in farm houses to give favourite beggars (who generally carry about the news of the country) a bowl or tin of broth in the kitchen, and the quality of the food was estimated just in proportion to its thickness. One day a beggar called at the house of a woman of a miserly ("near") reputation, who handed him a tin of very thin broth, and on her asking him: "Was it to his liking?" he said nothing. "Is it thick enough?" she enquired. "Well, mistress," he replied, "I got yen (one) grot (groat) and I see anither" (another).

5.—A clergyman in County Armagh once boasted he could preach a sermon from any text of Scripture. One of his congregation gave him the following: "Am not I thine ass?" The next Sunday he gave out as his text these words, as supplied to him. He first referred to the context, then dwelt on the meaning of the question, and, finally, made this practical application: "My hearers, some of you pay me four shillings and fourpence per annum, or one penny for every Sunday, and in return for this handsome remuneration, I preach once every Sabbath, marry you, baptize your children, visit you in sickness, and attend your funerals—am not I thine ass?"

6.—The same clergyman told me that in Paris, on the occasion of one of its great exhibitions, he lost his way one evening, and in his dilemma, not being able to speak French, he mounted the steps of a statue, and began to recite "Lochinvar." A crowd rapidly collected, and one of them, an Englishman, coming close to him asked him what in all the world did he want? "You, sir," he replied, telling him as he stepped down of his inability to find his residence. The Englishman was so amused that he entertained him hospitably at a cafe, and then saw him safe home to his hotel.

7.—Coming into hospital one day long ago I overheard a patient say to another: "Is your chicken soup thin?" The reply came at once: "Ay, the bird only walked through them," to which the first answered: "Maybe it was on stilts."

8.—On one occasion I remarked to a carman in a country town who sometimes drove me, on his telling me the horse was a new one, that it was like the one he had when I had last employed him. "Oh, sir," he replied, sorrowfully, "like's a bad mark among sheep!" and when he had gone a short distance I soon discovered how inferior the present was to the former animal. The subsequent history of this unfortunate animal may be best related in the owner's words, who, in reply to my asking him how the horse was doing, said: "Dear be thankit, he's dead. He tuk (took) an ating (eating) diabatis (diabetes) and near han' (hand) broke me keeping him goin' (going) wi' (with) hay and oats, and the more I giv him the poorer he got, till near the end he was as thin as a harra" (harrow).

Nowhere is the humour and wit of the northern province of Ireland encountered more markedly than at fairs. The natural desire of the seller to point out and exaggerate the good features of his animal, and on the other hand, the keenness with which the buyer dwells upon the defects of the same animal, both afford ample facilities for remarks—humorous, caustic, and mordant—all the more pointed from the fact that there is often an attentive audience of onlookers who thoroughly enjoy the scene. The best of good nature prevails, and no matter how amusing or depreciatory the sayings be that are bandied to and fro, it is rare for any quarrel to arise. Let me give a very few examples:

A gentleman took a rather good hunter, who, however, had a very bad colour (a light Canary yellow) to Ballyclare Fair, and on being asked "what he wanted for the horse?" named what was thought to be a rather high price—one hundred guineas. The countryman looked again critically at the animal, and then said: "I'll give you twenty pounds, but (after a pause) you must first paint him a dacent colour."

One day at Saintfield fair, a gentleman on the lookout for a horse saw one he fancied, and made enquiries about him from the owner, who was a native of County Down. "There," said he, handing him the halter, "try the horse as much as you like, but you'll buy him as he stands, for I'll give you no warranty, nor allow him to be examined by a vit." (vet.). The gentleman got his coachman to try the horse in the usual way, "galloping him for his wind," etc., and, as nothing seemed amiss, he became more pleased with the animal. "Why won't you let him be examined by a veterinary surgeon?" said the gentleman. "Because," said the owner, "he has two faults, and ye may just find them out yersel' as I did." Finally, after some further trials, the horse was bought, and after the money was paid the purchaser said: "You can't refuse now to tell me his faults?" "He has two," said the countryman; "first, if ye turned him out in a field all about your place couldn't (could not) catch him." "Oh, that's easy managed," said his new owner, "we'll always keep a slip (a sort of light winkers) on him. What's his other fault?" "The second fault is this," said his former owner, "when ye do get him, ye'll find he's not worth the catching."

On one occasion, after purchasing a horse, the man who owned him said to me: "I forgot to tell ye, sir, he has wan (one) fault."

"What's that?" I enquired. "He won't live long enough," he replied.

At the celebrated Moy fair, a countryman examining a horse said, on running his hands over the horse's knees: "That boy has been saying his prayers." "Oh, not at all," said the owner, "he's not your soort (sort=particular religious sect), he always prays stannin" (standing).

A man who was taking a cow to a fair was accosted by a countryman, who enquired how much he was asking for her. The owner named a high price, whereupon the other replied: "Get her shod." No statement—so laconic and so expressive in its meaning—could better convey the idea that unless he asked less he would have to go to a good many markets with his beast.

It is said sometimes that in the North of Ireland we are a very fighting, quarrelling race; but surely the following story shows how little those who bring this charge understand us. Two men were brought before a magistrate in a local court ("bench day") in a county town in Ulster, charged with fighting in the public street. As the evidence against one of the prisoners was not conclusive, he was ordered to be released, and the magistrate was about to sentence his co-prisoner to a fine, when the man who had been liberated addressed him as follows: "We were not fighting when the polis (police) tuck us." "What were you doing then?" said his worship. "We were just trying to separate one another," said the man.

A well-known medical man in an Ulster town (with whom I have been acquainted since my boyhood), one of the strongest personalities in his district, who was as resourceful in fighting the complications of disease as in dealing with the difficulties of every-day life, asked the sub-inspector or officer of the Royal Irish Constabulary—a young Englishman who had recently been appointed to the neighbourhood—to dine with him one Christmas. On returning from his round of visits on Christmas Eve his wife, greatly put out, told him that a well-known half-starved dog of a neighbour had entered the larder and had escaped, taking with him almost the whole of one side of the breast of a turkey, which was to form one of the principal dishes of their Christmas dinner. The doctor, as was his wont, made little of the occurrence, but early next morning a well-known character in the town (who it was alleged the police thought was not above poaching) brought the doctor a hare, and a portion of its flesh was carefully applied to fill up the gap made in the turkey by the dog. At the dinner (and never was there a more entertaining host) by a judicious application of white sauce, and by careful manipulating in carving by the doctor, nothing was noticed amiss with the turkey. In helping his guest, the doctor gave him a slice from each side of the turkey's breast, and the flavour was so unique that the young English officer—no mean sportsman—who had hunted and tasted wild turkey in his time, said he had never eaten such a beautifully-flavoured bird; and, naturally, being a comparative stranger in the district, asked what was the breed of this particular turkey. The doctor replied it was a peculiar species that he himself took great pride in, and that it was the result not of natural, but of artificial selection. As long as the officer was in that Ulster town, he would at times refer to the beautiful turkey, which was the chief dish on a particular Christmas night he had dined with the doctor.

On one occasion, after a consultation with an old and valued former pupil, he kindly asked me to have something to eat at his house before driving to catch the train for home. We sat down to an excellent repast—roast duck and cabbage—

but, unfortunately, the bird was not sufficiently cooked. On finding this my host complained to his old housekeeper, who was attending us, and who is quite a character, and she at once replied: "I don't think there are many people could catch, kill, and roast a drake all within an hour!" and as she was leaving the room where we sat, she said, with great sarcasm to me: "Purfessor (Professor), maybe they are smarter in your big town" (Belfast). In justice to the old lady, it is only fair to say that she did not, through a mistake, get sufficient time for her work, and further, as the doctor told me, she had a great liking for this particular bird, and resented having to kill it. Indeed, her feelings probably would have best found expression in the famous Irish ballad:

"His neck it was green, most rare to be seen,
　　He was fit for a queen of the highest degree:
His body was white, and would you delight,
　　He was plump, fat, and heavy, and brisk as
　　　a bee;
The dear little fellow, his legs they were yellow,
　　He would fly like a swallow, and dive like a
　　　hake,
But some wicked savage, to grease his white
　　cabbage,
　　Has murdered Nell Flaherty's beautiful
　　　drake.

"My treasure had dozens of nephews and cousins,
And one I must get or my heart it will break,
To keep my mind easy, or else I'll go crazy—
This ends the whole song of my beautiful drake."

In the neighbourhood of Strabane, two twin brothers resided who were so similar in appearance that even their friends could not distinguish them. One of them left the district, and at a subsequent period news came that he was dead. A countryman, shortly afterwards meeting the surviving brother in a fair asked him: "Are you yourself or the one that died?" The survivor replied it was his brother who had died, whereupon the countryman said: "I never knew the differ 'tween ye afore" (before).

On one occasion while being driven by a coachman of a well-known County Down gentleman, who has two capital matching carriage horses, I asked: "Which horse is this" (only one was in the machine)? to which the coachman dryly replied: "Oh! that's t'other (the other) one."

A clergyman walking along a country road overtook a man who was in vain trying to raise on to his back several sheaves of recently cut grass, tied together by means of a rope. With the aid of the clergyman, the countryman at length got his load on his back, and just before walking off, he turned to the good Samaritan, who had come to his assistance, and said, by way of thanks: "I'll have to give ye a day's hearing forenenst (opposite) this."

The Ulsterman, no matter what may be his religion or politics is essentially democratic in his tendencies, and this is often shown in the humour met with in the northern province. The following incidents will illustrate this:

1.—At a levee in Dublin Castle, a lady on attempting to enter by what is called the "private entree" door, was stopped by the policeman in charge, who happened to be from the North of Ireland. Much disgusted at his action, she said: "I must get in, I am the wife of a Cabinet minister." He replied at once: "I couldn't let you in, ma'am, even if you were the wife of a Presbyterian minister."

2.—A man was once talking to an Ulsterman about his ancestors, his grandfathers and great-grandfathers, and the wonderful deeds of valour they had done by sea and land for the State, when, after a long recital, the Ulsterman enquired: "Are they all living now?" to which the other replied contemptuously: "Oh, no!" whereupon the Ulsterman said: "Then you're no better than a growing pratie (potato), the best part of you is underground."

3.—There is an old ballad giving an account of a quarrel between an Ulsterman and a Spanish dignitary, whom he had offended. The injured

Spaniard, with an air of loftiness, informs his opponent that: "I am Don Guzman Pedrillo de Sota Murillo, of fair Seville town," to which the Ulsterman, breathing the northern spirit, replies: "Ye may be Don Guzzler O'Swillo, or whatever ye willo, but I'm Mattha Brown."

I have endeavoured, in a very imperfect way, to point out some of the peculiarities of the folk-lore of the people who live in the northern province of Ireland, with which all my life and all my interests are bound up. I have not, for obvious reasons, touched upon such debatable subjects as the political and sectarian opinions of the inhabitants of Ulster. We are all entitled to our individual views on such topics, and we each should be tolerant of the opinions of others who may differ from us, but in the desire to help, in every way, our beloved country, every true and patriotic Irishman can say:

"We're one at heart, if you be Ireland's friend,
Though leagues asunder our opinions tend;
There are but two great parties in the end."

ULSTERISMS.‡

I HAVE been much interested in the series of articles and letters in your paper on "Ulsterisms," and if you think the subject has not been exhausted, I should like to supply you with some more of those curious words and phrases, which seem to form a distinct feature of the dialect peculiar to the Northern province. Many of these "Ulsterisms" came, no doubt, from Scotland, but, as Lord Dufferin very wittily remarked recently in reference to another subject, while that country may have supplied the sayings as the raw material, they have been considerably altered and improved into the perfect article we now hear in daily use. Other "Ulsterisms" have no connection with Scotland; but this is what one would expect, considering the different places from which the inhabitants of Ulster have from time to time come. While you may encounter these "Ulsterisms" in Belfast, their birthplace is undoubtedly in the country districts, and it is to be hoped that the present regrettable trend of civilization from country to city life will not lead to their decadence. It is a great misfortune that no genius has arisen in Ulster, like Burns or Scott, to make its folk-lore classical.

No one has a better opportunity of noting

‡ Paper contributed to "The Northern Whig," Belfast, of May 8th, 1901.

these "Ulsterisms" than a doctor. It is a well-known saying for an Ulsterman to ask his medical adviser to "spend his opinion" on some member of his household who happens to be ill. What he conveys by this phrase is that the doctor shall make a careful examination of the patient, and then give his opinion as to the nature, treatment, etc., of the case. Shakespeare makes Othello say: "I will but spend a word here in the house, and go with you"; but the use of the word in a medical sense is, I think, peculiar to Ulster. While proceeding to visit the patient the doctor may be told by the Ulsterman that the member of his family who is ill (it may be his wife) has a "bad brash" (attack), or that she has a "touch of the weed" (also spelled "weid"), that is, a sudden febrile attack; or that the sick person has an "income" (in Ulster this is usually applied to a chronic swelling of the leg or arm, but it has a much wider application apparently in Scotland, for in his delightful book "Rab and His Friends," Dr. John Brown, brother of the present distinguished Professor of Chemistry in Edinburgh University, represents one of his characters as saying: "Maister John, this is the mistress; she's got a trouble in her breast—some kind o' an income we're thinkin'." No term could be more expressive than "income"—that is, something unusual which has "come in" to the part affected). The doctor may, however, be informed that the person he is going to see had, as the result of a severe wetting, "got a founder." (The use of this old word, as applied to a horse, is well known, but as used in the case of human beings it is common in Ulster.) The doctor may learn that the patient has the "rose" (a very old term for erysipelas, from its colour, resembling that flower). I have heard the same disease styled "St. Anthony's Fire" in the South of England, apparently because it looks a fiery colour, or because tradition said that persons suffering from erysipelas could be cured by a pilgrimage to the shrine of St. Anthony. If the patient is a child he may be "donsie" (Scotch for sick or ailing), or he may have an attack of "dwaums" (a sudden illness), or he may have the "gnarls" (chicken-pox), the spots being like knots or gnarls of wood; or the "chin-cough" (whooping-cough). This was originally "kink-cough," from an old word kink (Anglo-Saxon cincian, and Dutch kinken), which was used with two meanings—(1) to laugh loudly (one often hears in Ulster, "he kinked with laughter"), and (2) to gasp for breath, as in the spasms or kinks of whooping-cough. Fletcher says:

"It shall ne'er be said in our country
Thou diedst o' th' chin-cough";

while Smollett, in his translation of "Gil Blas," writes most graphically: "She ran to the assistance of the good man, rubbed his forehead, and clapped him on the back, as is practised with children when they have the chin-cough." It is a pity that the modern word "whooping-cough" has so much displaced the more ancient and classical term "chin-cough," still largely used in Ulster. Again the doctor may be told that the person he is called to see has received an injury in the "lisk" (the groin or flank). This is an extremely old English word, the same as the Danish "lyske." It is found in "Morte Arthure": "The laste was a litylle mane, that laide was be-nethe, his leskes atte lene and lathelicke to schewe"; or that he has a "gathering in his oxter" (the armpit, a word brought from Scotland, but originally derived from the Anglo-Saxon ohsta, the armpit). An infectious or catching disease is called "smittle," hence the Ulster proverb: "Mocking's catching, and gaunting's (yawning) smittle." The word gaunt (dialectal variant, gant), which is common in Ulster, is of Scotch origin, and there is a well-known saying in Scotland:

"Gaunting bodes wanting one of three,
  Meat, sleep, or good company."

In a church in Co. Down, on one occasion, after a very prolonged service, the minister gave out six verses of a Psalm to be sung. At the conclusion of the first verse the old precentor looked up at the clergyman and said: "I think, sir, that's enough, I see them (the congregation) gaunting."

During an illness the person is often said to be "under the harrow" (that is, the illness is a severe one). His friends hope "he has got the turn," but if the illness prove fatal, they will put it most expressively: "he's gone" (the Scotch is "he's awa' "). When a person dies he is said to be "underboard" from the time of his decease until his burial. In reference to the funeral those who wish to attend are "warned" for a certain hour, say twelve o'clock, but generally they "lift" (that is, the funeral starts) half an hour or an hour later.

Most expressive terms are employed descriptive of the people in Ulster. A child is a "back-gone wean" when it has lost its flesh; it is "reel-footed" if there is a club-foot; it is "skelly-eyed" if it has a squint (in "Old Mortality" it is used: "It is the very man," said Bothwell, "skellies fearfully with one eye"); it is "bandy-legged" if the legs are bent or bowed. This is a most interesting word in its origin. It would seem that about the time of Queen Elizabeth a game, the prototype of the modern tennis or hockey, came into vogue, and the stick or racket used in striking the ball was styled the "bandy." In his "Vision of Sin," Tennyson writes:

"To fly sublime
Thro' the courts, the camps, the schools,
    Is to be the ball of Time,
Bandied by the hands of fools."

The use of the word in the further sense of "give and take" is seen in "Lear," where Shakespeare uses it as follows: "Do you bandy looks with me, you rascal?" In Faulkland, in Fifeshire, the late Marquis of Bute spent thousands of pounds in restoring the old monastery, and I saw there a few years ago one of the best examples of these old tennis or bandy courts, which is said to be now as perfect as when it was originally built. The "bandy" club had a peculiar bend or crook at one end, and a person whose legs resembled this bandy club was said to be "bandy-legged." We find it in Swift:

"Nor make a scruple to expose
  Your bandy-leg or crooked nose."

A "lamiter" is used for a lame person or a cripple. In "Jane Eyre" Charlotte Bronte writes: "You have now no doubt friends who will look after you, and not suffer you to devote yourself to a blind lamiter like me." A deaf person is said to be "hard-a-hearing." When a child is sent a message to a farmhouse, and the residents do not know him, he is asked, laconically: "Who's owe you?" and, with the usual Northern reserve, he will reply "My da" (father), and, on being pressed as to who his father is, the child will often give the name and address of his parent in full—*i.e.*, "John Thompson, of the Causey." The addition of the place of residence serves to distinguish his father from all other men of the same name. (The word "Causey"—Causeway—is very common in Antrim and Down. It means a road raised above the usual level of the ground by stones. In "Paradise Lost" we have it employed by Milton:

"The other way Satan went down,
The causey to hell-gate.")

On the child explaining his parentage, the farmer or his good-wife will often reply: "Well, you don't favour your father's side of the house." (This word "favour"—to resemble—was used by Addison in the *Spectator*.)

The personal appearance of individuals is indicated by the following terms:—A dark-countenanced man is said to be "blackavised" (black of his visage). In "Jane Eyre" Charlotte Bronte writes: "I would advise her blackavised suitor to look out; if another comes with a longer or clearer rentroll he's dished."

As is well-known, that most remarkable genius, Charlotte Bronte was the daughter of a County Down man, who lived in the neighbourhood of Rathfriland, and it is interesting to find her employing in "Jane Eyre" such words as "lamiter" and "blackavised," which one may hear now every day in the district where her father spent his early life. On enquiring once from a countryman how his mother was, he replied pathetically: "Oh, doctor dear! She's clean dark" (blind).

A stranger going through a district is termed by the residents a "foreigner"; a stout man is "lusty"; a buxom-looking woman is "sonsy." In Scott's "Heart of Midlothian" we read: "Is she a pretty girl?" said the Duke; "her sister does not get beyond a good, comely, sonsy lass." A stupid person is a "kitterty" or a "galumpus"; one who is a silly talker is a "haverel." In "Hallowe'en" Burns uses it:

"Poor hav'ral Will fell aff the drift,
An' wandered thro' the bow-kail."

A rascal is a "rapscallion"; a miserly person is "wee," "close-fisted," "near," "near-be-gone"; a tall, badly-made lad is a "grawl," while a small, dwarfed creature is a "crowl" (two schoolboys in the neighbourhood of Ballymena while at play one day quarrelled, when the bigger of the two said to the other, who was a little fellow, with great contempt: "Ye crowl; the next generation of ye will be thrashing banes (beans) under a creepie"—a low stool); a fine-looking, tall man is "clever"; a person whose temper is easily roused is said to be "short in the grain," or "grulchy"; one who speaks with great caution is "mealy-mouthed"; and if one does not attempt to fight his own corner he is said to have made no "debate" for himself; one who is forward or interfering is contemptuously styled a "beddy" creature. A man of good mental capacity, who uses his powers of observation, is said to be "knowledgeable." Such a person could not be deceived readily, unless it was "unbeknownst" to him. A preacher is said to be "fosey" if he is pointless in his sermon; he is "fusionless" if his discourse is pithless, or if, as I heard a County Down man say of a clergyman, "he preaches powerful wake" (weak). "Fusionless" is a variant of the Scotch "fissenless." In "Old Mortality" Scott uses it: "I will not wait upon the thowless, thriftless, fissenless ministry of that man." A preacher who is *"vox et praetera nihil"* is said to "gulder." I once heard an Ulsterman say of a young clergyman, who had a loud, badly managed voice: "You could hear the gulders o' him a wheen (a few) of perches afore you came to the meeting-house green." If an Ulsterman be accosted by someone whose identity he has forgotten, he says, apologetically: "You have the advantage of me."

A most important event in the life of a young Ulsterman is naturally his marriage. If he is shy, or does not know the relatives of his young lady, he may ask a friend to accompany him, and this person is called a "blackfoot" (a sort of matchmaker, the male representation of the modern female "gooseberry." The word has been made classical by its use in Scott's "The Fortunes of Nigel"). Sometimes, after the young people are engaged, or "bespoke," there may unfortunately be a fall-out: then there is said to be a "kick-up" between them, and sometimes the quarrel cannot be "patched up," because one of the parties has taken a dislike to the other; if this is the case, it may be said: "she took a lasting scunner against him," or he was "clean scunnered of her." If, however, all goes well and a marriage takes place, the girl is "married on" so and so; and she is often described as "Jane Brown, by her mother's name, but she is married on William M'Cullough." The first Sunday after marriage the young people go to their own place of worship; it is said they "made their appearance," and in former years they were accustomed to go "linked" (arm in arm). On this most trying occasion the bride's appearance is very freely discussed. Some will report "she is quare and ould," or, in reference to her age "she would get no change out of a forty-shilling note," or she is "weezened" (dried up appearance), or "cruel ornery-looking" (very ordinary). (In Ulster this really means ugly.) I once heard of a person who appeared under such circumstances, and who had a long, badly-carried neck, who was described in this graphic way: "She had a neck on her as long as a goose's thrapple" (windpipe). If the bride turns out a success, the husband is congratulated on having met with a good "fitter"; if she is frugal, she is styled a "gatherer"; and if, as a result, an air of prosperity appears about their home, the people say there is a great "roughness" (plenty) about the house, or they have a "full place both in and out" (plenty inside, and a farm well stocked), and if they become rich, the people say they are "full o' gold." But, unfortunately, the wife may turn out to be a bad manager and the husband a failure, the house then gets a "through-other" appearance, and if, by and by, they are unable to "make ends meet," they become "stone-broke" (this is like the word "bed-rock," used by American Stockbrokers). In the end they may be "canted" out of their home. (This word "cant" is most interesting; it appears in old Spanish (encante), old French (encant), and Italian (incanto). Some authorities say it is derived from Latin words "in quantum"—to how much will you bid?—while others believe it is from incantare (from cantare), to "proclaim." It is met as early as the end of the twelfth century, and is used specially in Ireland. The Scotch equivalent is "roup." Swift is very fond of this fine, old word; he speaks of "two monks," in the time of William Rufus, "outvying each other in canting the price of an abbey." I have heard the word "cant" (for auction) used all over Ulster, and a famous Auctioneer, Murphy by name, who lived in Rathfriland many years ago, was called a "cant-master." Speaking of a "cant" reminds me of another expressive Ulster word—"sweetner"—applied to a person—generally a friend or neighbour of the man whose articles are being canted—who gives an occasional bid to keep up the prices. Of course such a practice is contrary to law, but it is often "winked at."

An Ulsterman uses most appropriate words to describe the weather. When it alters to bad weather he says it is "broke." A still summer day, without any wind, is termed "quate" (quiet); a dry, cold day, with an east wind blowing, which tends to "skin" the face, is "hasky" (variant of harsh); a day with a mizzling rain is "drauky." It was near Groomsport I first heard the word "gurly" applied by a Bangor carman to a stormy day. It is an altered form of "growly." It is an old word, and is used in "The Daemon Lover" (Child's Ballads), as follows:

"The clouds grew dark, and the wind grew loud,
     And the levin fill'd her ee;
 And waesome wail'd the snaw-white sprites
     Upon the gurlie sea."

The word "gurly" is also frequently applied to a growling dog. On one occasion, I remember, when passing a house, a cross dog ran growling after me, whereupon a man, who was leaning over the "half-door," said, with the most perfect Ulster naiveté: "Don't be unaisy, sir; he's a bit gurly, but he wouldn't bite unless he deemed (thought) you were mebbe (may be) a beggar."

The word finally came to be used of people, as "Don't look gurly" (cross).

Everyone knows what a "saft day" is, but far more expressive terms are in use to describe the degrees of severity in the amount of rain falling. If it is very wet, and you ask an Ulster carman is it still raining, he will likely reply: "It's not waiting to rain; it's just teeming," or he may inform you that it is a most "lamentable teem." When there is a heavy fall of snow there is said to be a "white world."

In some of the previous articles the writers referred to terms used in Ulster descriptive of drunkenness. I once heard a person, who was brought into the hospital in a hopeless state of inebriety, described by a policeman as being "blind drunk and paralytic"; and a Southern judge told me he was greatly puzzled on his first circuit in the North of Ireland by a witness saying, in reference to the plaintiff in a case, that he had seen him "oxter-cogged" from Omagh market. What was meant was that two friends supported (cogged) him, each with an arm under his "oxter." Had the judge been a student of Burns he would have been able to understand the expressive Ulster phrase "oxter-cogged," for, in "Meg o' the Mill,"

"The priest, he was oxter'd; the clerk, he was carried;
And that's how Meg o' the Mill was married."

The greatest difficulty is often met in Ulster Courts in getting witnesses to admit that either they or others were drunk. An Ulsterman on one occasion, after a great deal of cross-examination, could never be forced to say anything about a friend's condition beyond the fact that he had never seen him "absolutely drunk," whereupon the witty Judge O'Brien, who presided, said: "Did you ever see him relatively sober?"

The greatest compliment you can pay an Ulsterman is to say he is "downright dacent" (decent); and if he entertains his friends well, they will report that he "done the thing dacent." I have heard the word decent used in an odd sense at a funeral in the country. A man said to the brother of the deceased: "If your brother could only sit up in his coffin and see the dacent funeral he is having he would be powerful pleased." If an Ulsterman is not quite sure of a person he puts it this way: "I am jubous (dubious) of him"; and if he gives him a "nip," or "does" him in the sale of a horse, he says: "that boy's worth a-watching." A neighbour may, however, retort: "You got your desarvins (what you deserve) for being so saft" (simple).

Many words in Ulster, spelled alike, are used with totally different meanings. I have said a good-looking, tall man is styled "clever," but when the same term is applied to a clergyman it means that he is a good preacher. The "heel" of the hand is that part of the palm which becomes more prominent when the fingers are extended back towards the wrist; the "heel" of a loaf is the lowest part of the crust; the "heel" of the evening is the after-part; and to "heel" up a cart means to tilt it on its end. (The word in this sense is an old one, and was used originally of a ship, and so Cowper writes:

> "Eight hundred of the brave,
>   Whose courage well was tried,
> Had made the vessel heel,
>   And laid her on her side.")

An Ulster lad when at school gets his "tasks" (a more expressive word than lessons). Formerly he was punished with the "tawse," or "ratan" (a form of cane from Malay); and he disliked very much when the master of the school called him up to his desk for a "pandy" (this word is of singular origin. It would appear the hedge-schoolmaster was often fond of airing his Latin, so when he was about to punish a lad he said; "Pande palmam"— "hold out your hand"—and, finally, the phrase was shortened to pande-pandy).

A favourite source of amusement to an Ulster lad is a "cogglety-curry," or "shuggy-shoo," made by placing a plank across a barrel or log of a tree. When nicely balanced with boys of equal weight at each end it gives, by its up and down movements, a pleasurable exercise. A third boy sometimes stands in the centre of the plank and is called the "candlestick." I have heard no derivation of these words, except that they are examples of onomatopoeia. I intended to have added some Ulster proverbs, and to have said something to illustrate the humour of the Northern Province, which, while it resembles the Scotch in being dry and caustic, has also a Hibernian sparkle all its own; but I have already occupied too much of your valuable space. In conclusion, let me, in true Ulster fashion, wish "good fordher" (forwarder) to all those who are engaged in the interesting study of the language of our Northern Province.

www.ingramcontent.com/pod-product-compliance
Lightning Source LLC
Chambersburg PA
CBHW070811050426
42452CB00011B/1990